Lotus Notes Domino 8
Upgrader's Guide

What's new in the latest Lotus Notes Domino Platform

Tim Speed

Dick McCarrick

Barry Rosen

Bennie Gibson

Brad Schauf

David Byrd

Joseph Anderson

BIRMINGHAM - MUMBAI

Lotus Notes Domino 8
Upgrader's Guide

First published: December 2007

Production Reference: 1061207

Published by Packt Publishing Ltd.
32 Lincoln Road
Olton
Birmingham, B27 6PA, UK.

ISBN 978-1-847192-74-5

www.packtpub.com

Cover Image by Raghuram Ashok (raghuram@iiitb.ac.in)

Companies Copyright Notices and Statements

Although the authors and editors have attempted to provide accurate information in this book, we assume no responsibility for the accuracy of the information in this book. Lotus Domino 8 is a great product with many new features. Due to publishing deadlines parts of this book reference Beta code, including many screen shots. If you find an error, please let us know.

Warning and Disclaimer

Every effort has been make to make this book as complete and accurate as possible, but no warranty or fitness is implied regarding any information and/or products referenced in this book. Many of the authors, at the time of publishing, were employees of IBM. The IBM Corporation provides a set of rules regarding publishing that applies to each employee. The IBM employees followed each of these rules as stated by IBM. Based on those rules the following statements are listed:

- This book is not sponsored by IBM/Lotus or ISSL.
- The IBM employees received IBM legal permission to publish this book using an outside IBM Press publisher.
- Purchase and read this book at your own risk.
- Every effort has been attempted to obtain permissions for extracts and quotes when ever possible. See listed URLs for quote sources.
- The products referenced or mentioned in this book are listed for informational purposes only. The publisher and authors may have received demo copies to review. Many different vendors are mentioned in this book and many vendor products are used for reference. The publisher and authors do not recommend any product, software, or hardware. You, the owner of your hardware, software, and data are responsible to make a determination of what is best for you. The authors DO advise that you take careful consideration in determining your software; security and infrastructure needs and review more than just one vendor.

IBM

See this URL http://www.ibm.com/legal/copytrade.shtml

In no event will IBM be liable to any party for any direct, indirect, special or other consequential damages for any use of this book. all information is provided by the authors on an "as is" basis only. IBM provides no representations and warranties, express or implied, including the implied warranties of fitness for a particular purpose, merchantability and noninfringement for any information in this book.

Credits

Authors

Tim Speed

Dick McCarrick

Barry Rosen

Bennie Gibson

Brad Schauf

David Byrd

Joseph Anderson

Reviewer

Stephen Hardison

Senior Acquisition Editor

David Barnes

Development Editor

Nikhil Bangera

Technical Editor

Arnab Chakrabarty

Editorial Team Leader

Mithil Kulkarni

Project Manager

Abhijeet Deobhakta

Project Coordinator

Patricia Weir

Indexer

Monica Ajmera

Proofreader

Martin Brooks

Production Coordinator

Aparna Bhagat

Shantanu Zagade

Cover Designer

Shantanu Zagade

About the Authors

Tim Speed

Tim Speed is an IBM Certified Systems Architect with IBM Software Services for Lotus. In that capacity, he is responsible for designing, implementing, and supporting various engagements with its clients. Mr. Speed lives in Denton, Texas and has been an IBM/Lotus employee for over 12 years in a variety of networking, technical, hardware and software support and consulting positions. He has been working with Notes for over 15 years focusing on administration roles and infrastructure. He also has international experience with working on infrastructure engagements in Spain, Japan, Hong Kong, Singapore, Malaysia, the UK, and Indonesia.

Knowledge is based on many different facets - what you know, knowing where information can be found, and who you know. The information in this book is a combination of all these facets. Data sources have been referenced in this book, these include references to people, URLs, and other books. But much of the knowledge that is in this book comes from very smart people. Not all the people listed in this acknowledgement participated in the writing of this book, but have influenced and guided me in my life that has culminated in this work. First and foremost I need to thank my wife for helping me with the book and providing some of the editing throughout the various chapters. Next I want to thank Johnny and Katherine for tolerating me during the months that I worked on this book. Next I want to thank my mother, Lillian Speed, for teaching me to "think big." Thanks to Ed Speed for the inspiration to keep publishing. Thanks to Packt , David Barnes, Nikhil Bangera, and Patricia Weir for their hard work in getting this book published. The quality of the editing of this book is due to Dick McCarrick – one of the best editors in the business. Thanks to the various vendors for their submissions to the Appendix of this book

Thanks to all the co-authors – you ALL did a great job!

Special thanks to Lotus/IBM (and ISSL), Larry Berthelsen, Chris Cotton, Mark Steinborn, John Munnell, Dan Lorraine and Jack Shoemaker for their assistance in getter this book published. Thanks for Steve Hardison for reading this book before publishing. Many thanks to Mark J. Guerinot for writing the forward to this book.

Now to talk about the really smart people - due to legal issues, the people listed below did not directly contribute to this book, but I have learned a lot from these people via work and their friendship:

Gail Pilgrim, Jason Erickson, Jeff Jablonowski , John C.P. Allessio, Boris Vishnevsky, Adam Hanna, Brad Schauf, Scott Souder, David Byrd, Glenn Druce, Stan Logan, Paul Raymond, David Little, Craig Levine, Mark Harper, Jeff Pinkston, Jordi Riera, Dave Erickson, David Bell, Mark Leaser, Gary Wood, John Kistler, Jon P Dodge, Luc Groleau, Michael Dennehy , Robert Thietje, Francois Nasser, Kim Artlip, Marlene Botter, Mike Dudding, Stephen Cooke, Ciaran DellaFera, Tom Agoston, Carl Baumann, Dr Seshagiri Rao, Agustin "Gus" Richart, David Janes, Alistair Rennie, Amanda Vance, Andrea Waugh Metzger, Andy Higgins, Barry Rosen, Bennie Gibson, Beth Anne Collopy, Bill Hume, Brent A. Peters, Ivan Dell'Era, Butch Bantug , Carlos Gonzalez, Chad Holznagel, Charles K. DeLone, Dennis Weldon, Dale Sibley , Dolby Linwood, Don Bunch, Don Nadel, , Cheryl Rogers-McGraw, Tracy Goddard, Christopher Byrne, Chuck Stauber, Daniel Kill, Kurtis W Ruby, David Carno, David R. Hinkle, Doug Parham, Hobert Davis, David Davis, Dwayne Oliver, Todd Merkel, Kelly Ryan, The very smart Frederic Dahm, Gary Ernst, Gary Desmarais, Gary Palmer, Germaine Wales , Glenn Sicam, Henry Bestritsky, Traci Blowers, Hissan C Waheed, Ian Reid, James Wheeler , Jason Short, Jay Cousineau, Jayasree Gautam, Anthony (Joey) Bernal, Nancy Norris, Nancy Stevens, Dr. John Lamb, Robert Nellis, and special thanks to another very smart dude – "John Norton"; also thanks to: Jay Leiserson, John Sullivan, Joseph Anderson, Joyce Cymerman, Katherine Holden, Kathleen Kulkoski, Kevin Lynch, Michael Dudding, Lauri Jones, Lisa Santana, Marc Galeazza, Marco M Noel, Mark Leaser, Mark Steinborn, Marlene Botter, Mary Ellen Zurko, Naemi Engler, Nancy Stevens, Paul Culpepper, Paul Raymond, Peter Burkhardt, Ralph Vawter, Rena Chang, Nancy Norris, Rex McCaskill, Richard S Gornitsky, Rob Gearhart, Rob Sellati, Robert Nellis, Robert Thietje, Sean F Moore, Sean Long, Sean Scott, Sherry Price, Stephen Hardison, Steve Sterka, Steve Matrullo, Steven J Amadril, Tara Hall, Terry Fouchey, Victor Ross, William Destache, and the great Ted Smith.

Dick McCarrick

Dick McCarrick is a freelance writer who has worked extensively with Lotus Notes and Domino over the years. Dick spent over 15 years with the Lotus Notes and Domino team, initially as a documentation writer, then later with developerWorks: Lotus. Since leaving IBM, he continues to be involved with Notes/Domino, co-authoring three previous books on this product.

Barry Rosen

Barry Rosen is currently an Advisory IT Specialist with IBM Software Services for Lotus. During the last two years, Mr. Rosen has worked on several large messaging and migration projects as well as performed Domino upgrades and messaging assessments. Before that he was a Software Engineer in Lotus Support for over five years. While in support Mr. Rosen was on several teams specializing in mail routing, Lotus Notes Client, calendaring and scheduling, and server core. He focused on clustering, Lotus Notes for the Macintosh, and rooms and resources. Currently Mr. Rosen resides in Houston, Tx with his wife Micol, daughter Samantha, and Goldendoodle Stella. Having graduated from the University of Texas at Austin, Mr. Rosen enjoys following Longhorn sports.

There are so many people that I want to thank for their help. First, I would like to thank Packt Publishing, for publishing this book. Thanks to IBM where I have been allowed to grow personally and professionally. Dick McCarrick, who has helped to shape my words and ideas into something worthy of publishing. My manager, Larry Berthelsen, and Jack Shoemaker for approving this book, and all of their support. My co-authors who have poured countless hours and energy into making this book a reality. Tim Speed, with out whom this book would not exist. Tim, it seems like yesterday we were eating lunch in Rockefeller Plaza brainstorming on this book. Thanks for your patience and gentle nudging, you have helped me grow personally and professionally beyond my own expectations. My Mother, Father, brother, and gradparents. To all of my colleagues and friends: Mark Guerinot, Marc Galleazza, Chris Cotton, Gary Desmarais, Don Bunch, Luis Benitez, John Kistler, Bob Thietje, Glenn Sicam, Kelly Ryan, John Norton, Gail Pilgrim, Steven Amadril, Nancy Stevens, Carlos Gonzales, Matthew Buchman, David Carlston, Mike Noble, Todd Merkel, Tina Feuer, Chad Scott, Matt McCall, Kim McCall, Thu Doan, Michael Johannson, Bill McAnn, Larry Mancini, Keith Wooten, Stephen Hardison, Mark Harper, David Byrd, Joey Bernal, Marc Hendricks, Marc Allan, Matt Stien, Michael Granit, Stephen Rafoul, Seth Berk, Rob Buchwald, Aaron Greenberg, and Scott Sapire. Stella you too.

Bennie Gibson

Bennie Gibson is an IBM Certified Systems Architect with IBM Software Services for Lotus. In that capacity, he is responsible for managing various engagements with its clients. Mr. Gibson lives in Wake Forest, NC and has been an IBM/Lotus employee for over 24 years in a variety of sales, consulting, and management roles. He has been working with Notes for over 10 years focusing on architecture and infrastructure. He also has international experience with working on infrastructure engagements in Malaysia.

Thanks to Tim Speed for the opportunity to participate in the effort on this book.

Thanks to: Jeff Eisen, Jeff Calow, Niklaus Hiedlauf, and Brian O'Donovan.

For their expert input regarding Lotus Notes 8, SOA and the composite application editor. Thanks to my manager Dan Lorraine and our Director of Americas Mark Guerinot for supporting this valuable and important work in ISSL. And, finally, thanks to the extended team of ISSL consultants for their input and ongoing efforts in supporting leading edge products like Lotus Notes 8.

Brad Schauf

Brad Schauf is an IBM Executive I/T Architect with over 20 years of experience in the computer services and consulting industry. He has experience with enterprise-wide software and messaging and portal deployments, with a concentration on Lotus Notes/Domino messaging infrastructure architecture, application development, and integration as well as WebSphere portal architecture design and deployments. His experience includes API-level application development and lead programmer, enterprise lead for messaging and portal deployments to General Manager including P&L commitments. He was a founder of a successful IBM business partner before joining IBM in 1999.

I would like to thank everyone at IBM and (insert publisher name here) for allowing me the time and information required to write this book. IBM continues to be an amazing place to work filled with smart people.

David Byrd

David Byrd is an IBM Senior Certified Executive IT Architect with IBM Software Services for Lotus from Fayetteville, GA. He has been an IBM/Lotus employee for over 9 years in a number of consulting positions covering various technology areas. David has a deep background in virtually all areas of Lotus products and technologies covering areas ranging from low-level API development and collaborative application architectures, to security architectures and messaging architectures. His current focus is on Lotus Quickr as well as other team collaboration technologies and its deployment within enterprise customers. He has worked with Lotus Notes and Domino for over 15 years.

I would like to thank many people for their support in the creation of this book.

Thank you to Packt Publishing for providing me a formal venue to put down the thoughts running around in my head.

A special thanks to Dick McCarrick and Tim Speed for their efforts in putting this book together and inviting me to be part of the ride.

The next group is a set of very smart people that have been influential in the many areas covered in my section: Stephen Hardison, Mark Harper, Chris Heltzel, Gene Leo, Greg Melahn , Marc Pagnier, Satwiksai Seshasai, Tim Speed, Amy Widmer, and the ISSL Technology Team.

Finally I would like to close by thanking the ISSL management team for their support of this book and my involvement.

Joseph Anderson

Joseph Anderson is an IBM Certified Senior Managing Consultant from the IBM Software Services for Lotus team. Joseph has worked with Lotus Notes/Domino, Lotus Sametime, and Lotus QuickPlace since the early 1990s, primarily as a consultant. He is currently working with the Competitive Software team focusing on Domino/Notes administration, migration/upgrade, and security. Prior to working in the consulting industry, Joseph worked in the legal industry as a Director of Operations, where he leveraged his Master of Science in Legal Administration from the University of Denver College of Law.

I would like to thank the following individuals who helped me through the writing process, Andy Higgns, Tad Siminitz, and Rick Sizemore for contributing valuable content; Adam for his support and giving me the time to do the writing; Tim for including me as an author and to Dick for his tireless efforts in editing my content; my mom, brother, sisters; and finally my love to Kylie, Jacob and Jolie for being so patient with daddy.

About the Reviewer

Stephen Hardison is an IBM Certified IT Specialist with IBM Software Services for Lotus. He focuses on the design, implementation, and assessment of large-scale collaborative solutions based on Lotus Domino, WebSphere Portal, and Lotus Connections. Mr. Hardison joined IBM in 1999, and has worked in the Information Technology industry for over 20 years. He has worked on several world-wide deployments of Lotus products. Customer engagements have taken him to Argentina, the Bahamas, Brazil, Canada, France, Switzerland, and the United Kingdom. He lives near Austin, Texas.

Table of Contents

Foreword

The way information is exchanged is shifting, requiring companies to change how they manage their most important asset: knowledge. Increasingly, professionals are turning to on-line venues to communicate what they know and to create communities of collaboration. They are developing ad-hoc methods to collaborate and get work done. They are relying on email, instant messaging, and on-line, team-based, electronic user environments.

The latest release of IBM Lotus Notes and Lotus Domino reflects these developments — not only to support the way people work today, but to establish a foundation for a future of increasing collaboration. Lotus Notes is the premier integrated messaging and collaboration client option for the Lotus Domino server. Lotus Notes can help businesses enhance the productivity of their employees, streamline business processes, and improve overall responsiveness.

IBM Lotus Notes 8 supports previous Lotus Notes applications, while offering improved capabilities and delivering innovations in collaboration. The software will provide entirely new capabilities, including composite applications and office productivity tools that can help improve the way people work. In addition, Lotus Notes and Domino 8 software can play a key role as organizations adopt service-oriented architecture (SOA) strategies.

Lotus Notes 8 Enhancements

For the end-user, "at the glass" interactions are critical aspects of their daily lives. An interface that can improve the user's experience is critical to software adoption. However, learning new technologies must be intuitive. With the IBM Lotus Notes 8 client, IBM has delivered on these expectations. From the initial look-and-feel of the Notes client, to the full integration with the Sametime and Quickr platforms, IBM has accelerated the business value of the end-user experience with email and more.

Here are just a few of the enhancements that you'll see in the IBM Lotus Notes 8 release. These are designed to help your organization collaborate better and promote productivity and responsiveness.

Mail

IBM Lotus Notes 8 software continues IBM's commitment to helping you better manage information received via email, while also allowing you to work from within your inboxes. New mail features include:

- Threaded emails are gathered together and presented at the view level. You can easily expand a thread and see all messages related to specific topics grouped together. In preview mode, you can quickly find the information you are seeking, which is often hidden in long conversation threads.

- Really Simple Syndication (RSS) feed reader plug-in is accessible from the sidebar. You can scan information from your favorite news feeds and use it to answer questions and complete tasks. As with all the sidebar plug-ins, the RSS feed reader can be detached from the sidebar with the "float plug-in" option, allowing you to work in the way that you are most comfortable.

- Common keyboard and mouse-click shortcuts and commands are now supported. For example, you can use the Control key to select multiple, noncontiguous items in the Lotus Notes database view, which allows you to interact with multiple pieces of information simultaneously.

- Message recall capability allows you to retrieve email messages that have already been sent.

Calendar

New Calendar improvements enable you to manage your time and meeting invitations, and make decisions from your calendar, while reserving your inbox exclusively for email message management. Calendar enhancements include:

- Dates of important meetings or appointments are highlighted in the monthly calendar view. Highlighted dates on the monthly calendar give you a visual cue about days with scheduled meetings and unprocessed invitations. You can respond to unprocessed invitations by simply double-clicking on highlighted entries to accept, decline, or counter-propose an invitation.

- When scheduling conflicts arise, Lotus Notes 8 now allows the meeting chairperson to simply select or deselect attendees to find times that best meet the needs for that meeting.

Contacts

Contact functionality (previously called the personal address book) now offers a new user interface that helps boost productivity by enabling you to navigate contacts more quickly. Other new features include:

- Business-card-like views with embedded photographs help you find contact information more quickly.

- You can leverage the extensibility of Lotus Notes 8 software to initiate contextual collaboration from the Contact view.

- You can open individual contact information in a new window. If you prefer, you can easily change the view to traditional Lotus Notes tabbed views.

Service Oriented Architecture (SOA)

In addition to providing a world-class solution for messaging and collaboration, Lotus Notes and Lotus Domino 8 is an industry-leading, robust platform for developing people-centric applications. It helps you and the designers in your organization build applications that assist your people to be more productive and to meet your business requirements. The continued evolution of the Lotus Notes/ Domino platform allows it to participate openly within diverse IT environments, create new value from existing applications, and contribute to your service-oriented architecture (SOA).

Lotus Notes/Domino 8, through its support of user-facing composite applications and web services, provides new opportunities to evolve toward an SOA, while preserving your application and infrastructure investments. Your IT team can seamlessly introduce new application capabilities that help increase user efficiencies, through a familiar UI. The open, extensible Lotus Notes 8 model allows you to use development tools and component technologies that best align with your IT strategy, skills, and assets.

Using the Rest of This Book

Written by some of the senior architects and specialists of IBM Software Services for Lotus, this book will provide you with an excellent guide to help you realize the value of your investment in Lotus Notes 8. You will learn how to leverage the full capabilities of Lotus Notes 8 and how to quickly move from your existing technology base to this new, feature-rich platform. The authors explore the enhanced productivity tools available with this release, integrating word processing, presentations, and spreadsheets into a seamless unit with your messaging and collaboration solution.

Developers are not forgotten, as new features and tools are revealed. You will delve into the world of SOA, as the authors show you how Lotus Notes can be part of an SOA strategy that can accelerate your business integration and generate value. The book finishes with a few words about other Lotus products, such as Lotus Sametime, Lotus Quickr, Lotus Connections, and IBM WebSphere Portal—like IBM Lotus Notes, all built on the open-standards-based Eclipse Rich Client Platform (RCP) technology. These products are all converging to become the next generation of people productivity solutions.

Conclusion

Over the years, Lotus Notes has come to signify the essence of electronic business communications. With Lotus Notes 8, IBM has once again provided the user with an intuitive, fully integrated platform to enhance each user's experience with business communications. It is no longer just an email tool, but a basis to extend business communications to a new level.

I hope you find this book valuable as you continue your journey with IBM Lotus Notes and Lotus Domino 8.

Mark J. Guerinot

Director, Americas
IBM Software Services for Lotus (ISSL)
IBM Software Group

Preface

If you're reading this book, you're probably already familiar with Lotus Notes and the Domino server. You know about the powerful productivity features offered by this product and you know how much your company relies on it to communicate, collaborate, and manage its collective store of corporate knowledge. This book is intended to show you the new features of Lotus Notes and Domino 8. These outstanding products keep evolving with each release. This exciting new release will help your end-users with new features; but it will also help the administrator will new management features. This book has been written by Notes/Domino "insiders". Collectively, we possess decades of Notes/Domino experience; we've been with the product since Notes 1.0, and since then have worked directly with customers to help them with their Notes/Domino upgrade and deployment issues.

What This Book Covers

Chapters 1 and *2* will help you understand the new features in Notes client user interface and Domino 8.

In *Chapter 3* we introduce the concept of a Service Oriented Architecture (SOA) and how Lotus Notes 8 fits into one. You will get a high-level understanding of SOA, what it is, its value, and its characteristics. You will also learn how Lotus Notes 8 has many of the characteristics of SOA components, and how it can help you assemble applications that can play a role in an SOA.

Chapter 4 provides an overview of three productivity tools: IBM Lotus Documents, IBM Lotus Presentations, and IBM Lotus Spreadsheets. You will how these tools are integrated with Notes 8, and how they are controlled by Domino policy documents.

Chapter 5 takes a look at the major new and enhanced feature areas in Domino 8. This includes end user and messaging enhancements, administrator enhancements, performance enhancements, directory and security enhancements, and better integration with other IBM technologies.

In *Chapter 6* we examine important Notes/Domino 8 features that can make rolling out your new deployment significantly easier. We discuss client provisioning, including Eclipse-based client and server provisioning functionality. We also look at policy enhancements and the new database redirect feature.

Chapter 7 is divided into two main sections. The first takes a look at the Notes/Domino upgrade process in general, discussing concepts and steps that should be considered whenever you upgrade to any major release of Notes/Domino. The second section covers upgrade issues that are specific to Notes/Domino 8.

In *Chapter 8*, we examine coexistence issues involved with running Notes/Domino 8 in a mixed environment with one or more previous releases. We begin with a look at Notes client coexistence considerations, explain how to install two different versions of Notes on a workstation, and discuss potential issues with calendaring and scheduling in a multi-release environment. The chapter concludes with a discussion of Domino 8 server coexistence, including features such as Domino Directory, ODS, Domino Web Access, DDM, and ID files.

In *Chapter 9*, we review some of the major new features and enhancements that affect Notes/Domino 8 application development. These include enhancements related to composite applications, Domino Designer 8, formula language and LotusScript, Lotus Component Designer, Web 2.0, and Lotus Expediter.

Chapter 10 discusses add-on products for a typical Notes/Domino infrastructure. The specific products covered in this capture are the most common that you might encounter, including: Lotus Quickplace/Quickr, Lotus Sametime, and Lotus Connections.

The *Appendix* covers vendor offerings that will help you extend your Lotus Notes/Domino 8 environment. The tools covered are PistolStar's Password Power 8, IntelliPRINT Reporting, IONET Incremental Archiver and CMT Inspector.

Conventions

In this book, you will find a number of styles of text that distinguish between different kinds of information. Here are some examples of these styles, and an explanation of their meaning.

There are three styles for code. Code words in text are shown as follows: "Call the Java agent, again using the NotesAgent `RunOnServer` method and passing the document `NoteID`."

A block of code will be set as follows:

```
public void NotesMain() {
    try {
        Session session = getSession(); //Instantiate NotesSession
```

New terms and **important words** are introduced in a bold-type font. Words that you see on the screen, in menus or dialog boxes for example, appear in our text like this: "Click the **New Web Service** button to create a new web service".

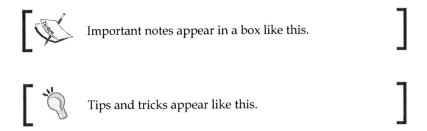

Important notes appear in a box like this.

Tips and tricks appear like this.

Reader Feedback

Feedback from our readers is always welcome. Let us know what you think about this book, what you liked or may have disliked. Reader feedback is important for us to develop titles that you really get the most out of.

To send us general feedback, simply drop an email to feedback@packtpub.com, making sure to mention the book title in the subject of your message.

If there is a book that you need and would like to see us publish, please send us a note in the **SUGGEST A TITLE** form on www.packtpub.com or email suggest@packtpub.com.

If there is a topic that you have expertise in and you are interested in either writing or contributing to a book, see our author guide on www.packtpub.com/authors.

Customer Support

Now that you are the proud owner of a Packt book, we have a number of things to help you to get the most from your purchase.

Downloading the Example Code for the Book

Visit http://www.packtpub.com/support, and select this book from the list of titles to download any example code or extra resources for this book. The files available for download will then be displayed.

The downloadable files contain instructions on how to use them.

Errata

Although we have taken every care to ensure the accuracy of our contents, mistakes do happen. If you find a mistake in one of our books—maybe a mistake in text or code—we would be grateful if you would report this to us. By doing this you can save other readers from frustration, and help to improve subsequent versions of this book. If you find any errata, report them by visiting http://www.packtpub.com/support, selecting your book, clicking on the **Submit Errata** link, and entering the details of your errata. Once your errata are verified, your submission will be accepted and the errata are added to the list of existing errata. The existing errata can be viewed by selecting your title from http://www.packtpub.com/support.

Questions

You can contact us at questions@packtpub.com if you are having a problem with some aspect of the book, and we will do our best to address it.

To Linda Speed - my loving split apart
- Tim Speed

I would like to dedicate this book to my family who has offered their incredible support and patience to me. My wife Micol, and my daughter Samantha you are my world and I love you both dearly.
- Barry Rosen

This chapter is dedicated to my wife Gwen who has patiently waited through "one more chapter", "one more problem to fix", "one more conference call" or "one more e-mail to answer" for 30 years.
- Bennie Gibson

To my Bride Suzie and my two wonderful kids, Shelbie and Nathan. Also to my Mom and Dad who showed me the right way.
- Brad Schauf

I would like to dedicate my section of this book to my wife, Lorrie Byrd, and children, Ronan and Aidan Byrd, for their continual love and support both at work and in life.
- David Byrd

I would like to dedicate my efforts toward this book to Lisa, my loving wife and best friend, and to my father, Gary, who without knowing it led me to technology and ultimately my career.
- Joseph Anderson

1
A Short History of Notes and Domino

As with all great ideas, Lotus Notes started out as the solution to a specific need. Three programming students attending a Midwest university in the late 1970s wanted a way to share notes and information. To do this, they used a software program called PLATO Group Notes, which ran on their mainframe-based college computer system. This program really wasn't intended for this purpose—it was originally designed for bug reporting, but it did provide just enough communication and collaboration functionality to offer a hint at what could be done, given the right software and technology.

After graduation, these three students—Ray Ozzie, Tim Halvorsen, and Len Kawell (names that have since achieved near-legendary status within the Lotus Notes community)—went their separate ways. But none forgot the potential they saw in PLATO Group Notes. Halvorsen and Kawell took jobs at Digital Equipment Corporation, where they eventually created an in-house communication tool that resembled PLATO. Meanwhile, Ozzie took programming positions with other corporations, but never lost sight of his vision to form his own company and develop a more advanced, PC-based collaboration program. Eventually (1984 to be exact), with funding provided by the Lotus Development Corporation (makers of the famous Lotus 1-2-3), Ozzie founded Iris Associates Inc. to develop the first release of Lotus Notes. Ozzie was soon joined by former classmates Halvorsen and Kawell, and shortly thereafter by Steve Beckhardt.

This first version of Lotus Notes was modelled on PLATO Group Notes, but was far more advanced, sporting powerful features such as online discussion, email, phone books, and document databases. This functionality presented some serious challenges to the hardware and supporting infrastructure upon which Notes ran at the time. To meet these challenges, Notes was built upon then radical client/server architecture, which featured PCs connected to a **local area network (LAN)**. Groups set up a dedicated server PC that communicated with other servers. These servers exchanged information through **replicated data**, a concept familiar to us today, but extremely revolutionary at the time. This allowed users to exchange information with co-workers (however remote), while maintaining high performance. Equally important, Notes, from the outset, was designed to be highly customizable, with a state-of-the-art multi-faceted programmatic interface that allowed developers to create powerful applications specifically suited to the needs' of their work groups.

The first release of Notes shipped in 1989. (A five-year development cycle may seem like a long time by today's standards, but bear in mind that the Iris folks were basically creating an entirely new genre of software.) Release 1.0 provided several "ready to use" applications such as Group Mail, Group Discussion, and Group Phone Book. Notes also provided templates that assisted developers in the construction of custom applications, which led to a vibrant business partnership. Release 1 features included:

- Email.
- Advanced security features. These included the now-familiar Access Control Lists (ACLs), which control many aspects of Notes database access. Other security-related features included encryption, signing, and authentication using the RSA public-key technology.
- Dial-up functionality.
- Import/export capability, including Lotus Freelance Graphics metafile import, structured ASCII export, and Lotus 1-2-3/Symphony worksheet export.
- Online help (a novel idea at the time!).
- Formula language for programming Notes applications.
- DocLinks that allowed users to navigate from one Notes document to another, via technology that resembled an early form of today's URLs.
- Central administration.

Notes 2.0 shipped in 1991. By now, it became apparent that much of Notes' early customer base consisted of large companies that employed thousands of users. These companies were particularly intrigued by Notes' ability to bring large numbers of users together, and allow them to collaborate and share information with the speed and efficiency of a small, tightly focused team. To accommodate these customers, the Notes development team paid special attention to scalability enhancements, taking advantage of recent hardware and networking advances that could support large, geographically dispersed environments. These scalability features included support for multiple name and address books. In addition, the addition, the new Notes C applications programming Interface (API) enhanced Notes' extensibility, allowing experienced programmers to create more advanced custom application. The formula language was also extended. On the user side, Notes now supported rich text as well as tables and paragraph styles, and Notes mail was enhanced with such things as address lookup.

Notes 3.0 shipped in mid-1993. At this point, the installed customer base for the product had grown to approximately half a million users worldwide – substantial, but still orders of magnitude smaller than today's global Notes/Domino community. To help broaden its appeal to new markets, Notes 3.0 offered client support for the Apple Macintosh and server support for Microsoft Windows. Notes 3.0 also introduced many now familiar features, including full text search with hierarchical names, and alternate mail. Replication was enhanced so that users could perform selective replication, and run replication in the background.

It was around this time that the Internet began to be seen as a serious business tool, rather than merely the domain of students and socially inept "geeks". This led to the release InterNotes News, a product that provided a gateway between the Internet news sources and Notes. Although largely forgotten today, this was the first project that reflected the increasing need for Notes to work together with the Internet.

In January 1996, Lotus released Notes 4.0, offering a radically redesigned user interface that simplified many Notes features, making it easier to use, program, and administer. This interface quickly became popular among users and developers. The product continued to become faster and more scalable. In addition, Notes began to integrate with the Web, and many new features reflected emerging Web technology. For instance, the new Server Web Navigator allowed the Notes servers to retrieve pages off the Web so that users could view them in a Notes client.

Release 4.0 included something for everybody. As we mentioned, the user interface was completely re-engineered, offering the familiar three-paned UI (with preview capability) for mail and other applications. This UI is still available today in the Notes workspace. Users also took advantage of the enhanced search features, which included the ability to search non-indexed databases. Programmers welcomed the introduction of LotusScript, a programming language built into Notes, as well as new view, folder, and design features. Administrators also had a lot to cheer about. For example, the introduction of "pass-thru" servers made it much easier to built network topologies that ensured quick and efficient delivery of email. Server integration with the Internet was improved, including SOCKS support, HTTP proxy support, and Notes RPC proxy support.

In July 1995, IBM purchased Lotus. This gave the Notes developer team access to world-class technology, including the HTTP server now known as Domino (which eventually led to the Notes product being known by the current name Notes/Domino). This helped transform the Notes 4.0 server into an interactive web applications server, combining the open networking environment of Internet standards and protocols with the powerful application development facilities of Notes. Domino allowed customers to dynamically publish Notes documents to the Web—a major development in the life of the product.

Among the major enhancements offered in release 4.5 was calendar and scheduling. (It's hard to believe it hasn't been in the product all along.) To further the theme of Web integration started with Notes 4.0, release 4.5 also included a personal Web navigator, as well as seamless Web access from the Notes client. Scalability and manageability were improved with support for Domino server clusters and directory assistance. Security enhancements, such as execution control lists, and password expiration and reuse, helped give users more control over who could access their PCs and what could be performed on them. For the programmers, Notes 4.5 introduced script libraries.

Notes and Domino release 5.0 shipped in early 1999. The release continued the Notes/Domino integration with the Web to the point where the two technologies were essentially melded together. This was reflected in the release 5 interface, which bore a more browser-like feel. It also supported more Internet standards and protocols. Release 5 also introduced **Domino Designer**, the third member of the Notes/Domino triumvirate of products. And the new Domino Administrator made Domino network administration easier.

Domino 5 featured Internet messaging and directories, expanded web application services (including CORBA), and database improvements, such as transaction logging.

The Notes 5 client included a new browser-like user interface with a customizable welcome page for tracking daily information. It also included improvements to applications such as mail, calendar and scheduling, web browsing, and discussions.

By the time Notes 6 and Domino 6 were introduced in late 2002, industry talk focused on concepts such as lower total cost of ownership (TCO for the buzzword-inclined), increased productivity, and faster deployment.

In response, Domino 6 offered enhanced installation, scalability, and performance. Domino Designer 6 allowed developers to create complex applications more easily and to reuse code. And IBM improved the Notes 6 client, with an eye towards improving each user's personal productivity. The overarching theme was to help customers work more efficiently. For example, installation and setup offered more options and an improved interface. IBM made central management of multiple remote servers easier, through features such as policy-based management. And they improved server scalability and performance, with new features such as network compression and Domino Server Monitor. These themes were carried through Notes/Domino 6.5, which offered enhanced collaboration with tighter integration with Sametime instant messaging, QuickPlace, and Domino Web Access. For programmers, Release 6.5 included the Lotus Domino Toolkit for WebSphere Studio, a set of Eclipse plug-ins that can be used to create JavaServer Pages (JSPs) using the Domino Custom Tags.

Notes/Domino 7, released in 2005, continued the themes of ease of use, easier maintenance and deployment, and tighter integration with standards. For example, Notes 7 included usability features such as the ability to close all open windows with a single click, the ability to save the state of your work, and a prompt when the user sends a message with no subject. New client follow-up actions helped with messaging tracking and work flow, and new Mail rules provided for better spam management. For those looking for a quick status on digital message signatures and encryption, there were new status bar icons. Calendar and Scheduling (C&S) included a new calendar clean-up action that helps the end user to quickly and easily maintain calendar entries. In addition, end-users could now configure the calendar to accept a meeting, even if it conflicted with an earlier meeting. Notes 7 also offered enhanced presence awareness based upon Lotus Sametime, including the ability to see a person's name in a document or view and determine if that person is online. Presence awareness was added to team rooms, discussions, "to do" documents, personal name and address book, rooms and resources templates, and various C&S views.

In Domino 7 administration, Domino Domain Monitoring (DDM) was a particularly important new feature. Other features and tools included administration event script handling (via LotusScript), enhanced policy administration (including the ability to lock down end user desktops, and a new Mail policy), and integration with the Frivolity Autonomic Monitoring Engine (TAME). Enhancements to Smart Upgrade included the ability to detach kits in the background, to prevent time lost to a non-working client; and fail-over from a shared (network) upgrade kit to another server's attached kit. DB2 Management tools let you enable Domino to run with a DB2 data store, configure a connection document from DB2 Access for a Domino server to Domino, and allow DB2 user names and passwords to be added to server IDs.

The Domino 7 server offered autonomic diagnostic collection, a feature that can be considered both an administration feature and a server feature. It also included more improvements to directories and LDAP—for example, support for Universal Notes IDs (UNID) through 32-character values of the new dominoUNID operational attribute. LDAP searches were enhanced to work with IBM Workplace products that use the WebSphere Member Manager (WMM) service to access user and group objects. To optimize performance, Domino 7 re-used existing LDAP connections. IPv6 protocol support was upgraded to include additional platforms and services. Domino 7 also centralized the processing of Rooms and Resources reservations into a new Rooms and Resources Manager (RNRMgr) task. Additionally, it offered improvements with the Lightweight Third Party Authentication (LTPA) scheme.

Domino Designer 7 provided new features meant to help the developer better manage Notes/Domino applications, provide new user interface elements, as well as provide better support for newer technologies such as Web Services. For instance, the new Auto Save feature backed up any documents open in edit mode to a defined "auto save" database. Shared columns provided a mechanism to reuse a view column definition across multiple views. This allowed for consistency when sharing them among views. Agent profiling allowed developers and administrators to collect performance data for a LotusScript or Java-based agent. Input enabled formulas allowed you to define whether or not a field is editable using a "@Formula" that evaluates to @True or @False. Designer 7 provided several new smart icons, including Debug LotusScript.

As for Notes/Domino 8: well, its features are the subject for the next chapter. Let's just say for now that this latest release continues the tradition of cutting edge technology and functionality built into that first release, the culmination of three forward-thinking students who (not to wax overly dramatic) launched an entirely new software industry, and with it a whole new way of doing business, based on communication, collaboration, and sharing and managing the collective expertise of your corporation. In short, getting the most out of *all* your resources, hardware, software, and (most important of all) human!

2

Overview of New Lotus Notes 8 Client Features

In this chapter, we will take a quick look at some of the major new features offered in the Lotus Notes 8 client. These include:

- User interface enhancements
- Mail enhancements
- Calendar enhancements
- Contacts (formerly known as the Personal Address Book)

In addition to these "user visible" features, the Lotus Notes 8 client is now built upon an open standards Eclipse-based architecture. This architecture allows greater flexibility of the client for customization and fits better into a service-oriented architecture (SOA) than previous releases.

Lotus Notes 8 also provides a more consistent experience across a greater variety of operating system platforms. For example, The Lotus Domino 8 server software runs on Red Hat Enterprise Linux 5. Lotus Notes 8 client support for Red Hat Enterprise Linux 5 WS is currently planned for the Lotus Notes 8 code stream. The Notes 8 client also offers a consistent installation process for both the Microsoft Windows operating system users and Linux desktop users.

Enhancements in Lotus Notes 8 for Linux include integrated instant messaging and presence awareness, the Lotus Notes **Smarticons** toolbar, and support for color printing.

Lotus Notes 8 support for the Macintosh workstation will be expected at a later date.

In this chapter, we will discuss the enhanced UI and updates to mail, calendar, and contacts.

User Interface Enhancements

Long-time Notes users will notice that the Lotus Notes 8 user interface looks significantly different from previous releases. These changes are the result of carefully considering and incorporating user feedback and suggestions.

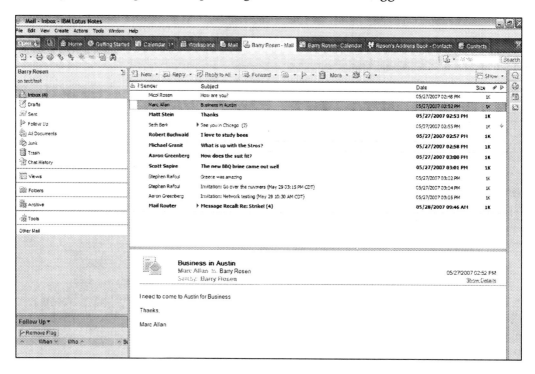

Welcome Page

Lotus Notes 8 has a new default Welcome page. The name of this page has changed to **Home Page**.

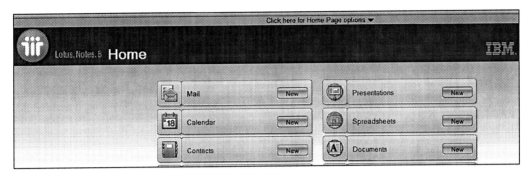

This page can be considered a "home base" from which to jump to your desired destination. It contains links labeled **Mail**, **Calendar**, **Contacts** (previously known as the personal address book), **To Do**, and **Personal Journal**. In addition to these familiar links, there are links to other productivity tools. For more details on these, see chapter 4, *Productivity Tools*.

As in previous releases of Notes, you can customize this page or create your own.

 Upgrading from a previous release of the Notes client will retain your existing welcome page.

Open List Menu

Lotus Notes databases are now called **spplications** in the Notes 8 client. There is also a new method to access them. To do this, click on a new menu button called **Open.** This button is located in the upper left-hand corner of the client interface.

From this menu, you can access the same links as from your default home page, as well as some additional links.

 Bookmarks from previous releases will be migrated if the client is upgraded to Lotus Notes 8 from a previous release. The workspace page is also still available as well.

A feature that is very helpful is the search feature in the **Open** menu. When entering text in this search, the **Open** menu will contextually adjust to show only the contents of your search.

The **Open** menu does not replace the **File** menu. Speaking of which, the **File** menu has been slightly modified. As mentioned earlier, the word "Database" has been replaced by "Application" in the menu options. There are also a few new icons such as a printer next to the **Print** option:

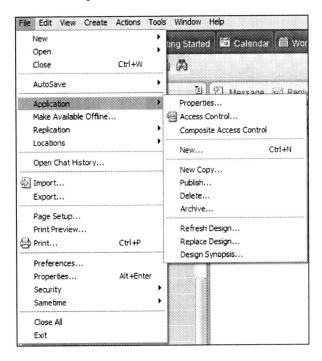

Toolbars

Lotus Notes 8 features contextual toolbars. Toolbars are now related to the tab of the application that is being used. Contextual toolbars allow only the tools that are necessary to be displayed.

Unified Preferences

With all these new features come associated new preference settings, some of which we have already mentioned. In Notes 8 the preferences are all in a single location. This makes the management of this feature-rich client simpler, because you can find the preferences for mail, activities, instant messaging, and productivity tools under one location.

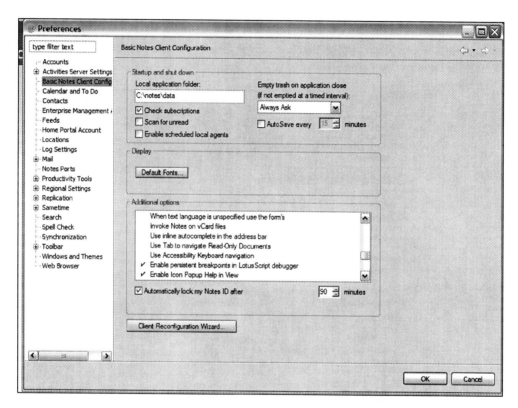

As with the **Open** menu and the **Thumbnail** view, in **Preferences** you can contextually search for preference settings. Notice a pattern here?

 If you are used to using the preferences in the same manner as the previous releases, you can do so in the Lotus Notes 8 client as well.

Windows Management and Tabs

To provide a less cluttered window, Lotus Notes 8 has enhanced the functionality of its windows and tabs.

Group Document Tabs

Lotus Notes 8 introduces the ability to group document tabs. With this option enabled, documents or views opened from within one application are grouped under the originating application tab.

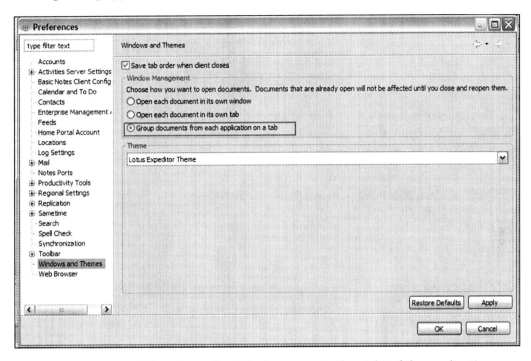

To access an open window in a tab, click the arrow to the right of the application name. The number next to the arrow displays the number of open windows within the parent application.

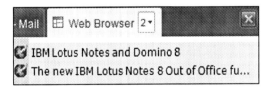

You can also now choose to have a new window open for every document.

Thumbnails

To the immediate right of the **Open** menu is the new **Thumbnails** button. Clicking on this button transforms the open windows into a page that contains each window displayed as a thumbnail. Clicking on a thumbnail image will take you to that window.

This feature is extremely helpful when you are dealing with multiple open windows. As in the **Open** menu, there is a contextual search available in the thumbnail view.

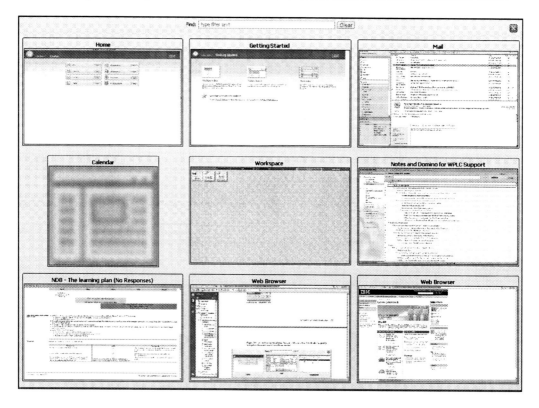

Advanced Menus

There is an old rule in the software business that states 80 percent of the users only use 20 percent of the features. If you are not a power user, and would rather not see all of the advanced menu options, just turn them off. In the Notes 8 client, if you fall into the 80 percent group, you never need to see these options. By default, the option of showing advanced menus is deselected. If you need to use an advanced menu, you will need to enable this option.

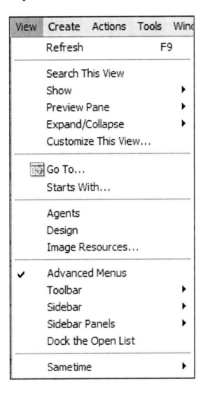

We can now see how the menus look with **Advanced Menus** enabled and disabled.

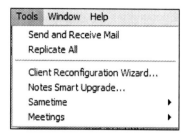

Offline Applications

Ever wish there were a simple way to create a local replica of an application? That is exactly what the new Make Available Offline feature does. Just select this option, enter the necessary information, and voila! a local replica of your application is created.

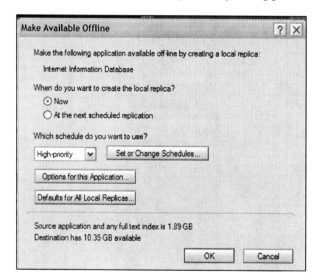

Search Center

The ability to search mail, calendar, contacts, and even the web from a single location is now a feature of the Notes 8 client. Both Google and Yahoo! Internet searches can be selected from within the client. Got Google Desktop search? If you have, it will also appear in the menu.

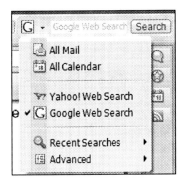

Searches can be saved as well. Using the search preferences, you can disable the search history, clear the search history, and choose which web search you want to set as your default.

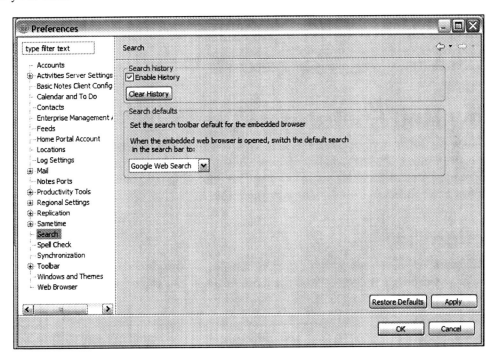

IBM Support Assistant

How much time could you save if you had your own personal support assistant when you run into a challenging issue? IBM responded to that wish by creating the IBM Support Assistant. The Support Assistant allows you to troubleshoot your issue without needing to contact IBM. If you can't resolve the issue with the Support Assistant, it will help by automating the process of collecting the diagnostic data needed to create a problem report.

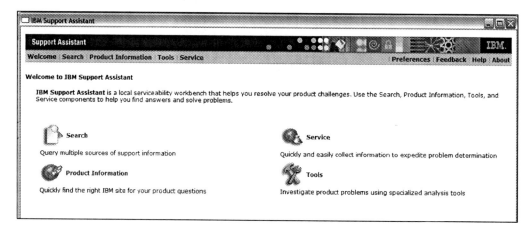

For more information on the IBM Support Assistant, see the Lotus Notes 8 client online help or the following web site:
`http://www.ibm.com/software/support/isa/`.

New Mail Features

The new mail functionality in the Lotus Notes 8 client was designed with the end user in mind. The enhancements were designed to simplify and update the interface, as well as increase productivity. The following sections cover the new mail functionality introduced in the Lotus Notes 8 client.

Action Bar

The appearance of the action bar has been modified from previous versions. If the new look confuses you, hover over the icon for a text box description of the icon's functionality.

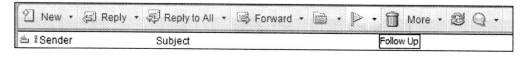

For basic functions (such as creating a new memo or replying to a message) you can click once on the icon. Notice the arrows next to the action bar items. Clicking on the arrows allows you to choose more options such as **Reply without history** or **Create a new meeting**.

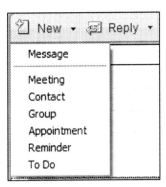

Show Menu

A new menu called **Show** now appears in the upper left-hand corner of the Notes 8 client interface.

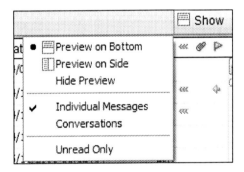

From this menu, you can alter the way your client displays your documents. One of the options in this menu controls how Notes displays the preview pane. We detail these options in the next sections.

Horizontal and Vertical Preview Panes

As mentioned previously, you can choose how to display the preview pane. The two options allow you to preview on the right or on the bottom. This fits into the philosophy of being able to customize the client's experience.

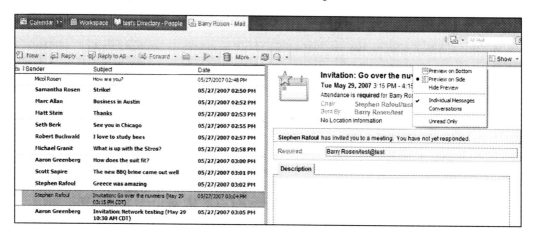

If you choose to display the preview pane on the right, the text of your messages will resize so that they fit in the preview pane. This allows you to view the same information regardless of the preview pane selection. The other option is to remove the preview pane altogether.

Mail Threads

Lotus Notes 7 allowed you to view the mail thread in the header of the email. Lotus Notes 8 builds upon this mail thread functionality. There are now two new options for mail threads when viewing directly from the inbox. By default, when you highlight a message in the inbox, it will display a twisty next to the subject if the message is in a thread.

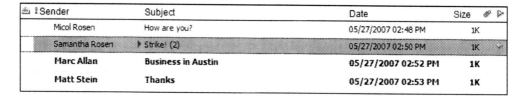

To see the contents of the entire mail thread, click this twisty.

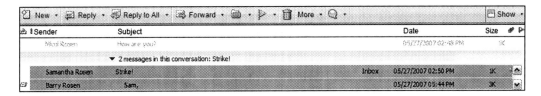

In most cases, replies to an email contain the original subject line preceded by **Re:**. The mail thread functionality in Lotus Notes 8 displays the first line of the email rather than the subject. This allows the user to scan the thread for useful information without having to open a memo to see the contents.

The mail thread will display all messages in a thread, regardless of the location of the actual message. If you move a message in the thread to any folder other than the inbox, the thread will display the name of the folder containing the message.

By making the mail threads resilient, the Lotus Notes 8 client will still display messages in the thread even if one of them is deleted. It also displays messages that originated outside of your Lotus Domino environment. If someone sends messages to you from the Internet, those messages are displayed in the thread.

 The mail file must be hosted on a Lotus Domino 8 server in order for the mail threads to be resilient.

Conversations View

Notes 8 allows you to display your messages in a **Conversations** view. This compacts emails to one message per conversation. This view provides an uncluttered inbox. The emails in a topic will be grouped together by the latest entry in your inbox. To switch between the conversations view and the individual messages view, use the **Display** menu.

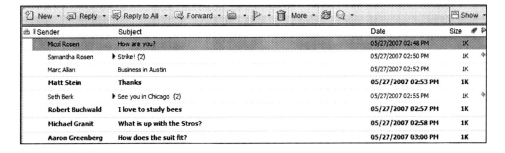

In the **Conversations** view, you will see the number of emails in the conversation in parenthesis at the end of the subject. Clicking on the twisty will display the messages in the conversation, just as it does in the default mail view.

Another time-saving feature in this view is the ability to perform actions on the entire conversation. These actions include filing into a folder or deleting the entire conversation. To prevent accidental deletion of an entire conversation, a dialog box will appear when someone deletes a conversation.

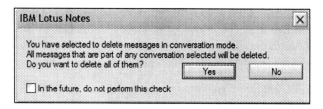

 This dialog box can be suppressed by checking a box.

Mail Header Options

If you only want to display the header options that are pertinent to you, now you can. In Notes 8 you can choose what header options to display in your mail file.

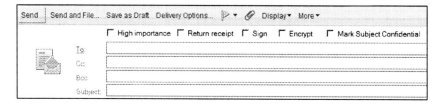

This figure displays all of the options in the mail header.
To limit the header options, click on the display button in the memo. This will allow you to choose what options to limit. You can hide everything except the **To, Cc,** and **Subject** fields.

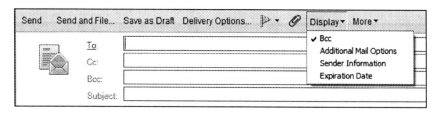

Sending confidential messages is easier in Notes 8. There is a check box named **Mark Subject Confidential**. When you check this option, the text ***Confidential** is added to the beginning of your subject.

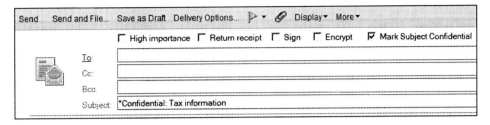

Mail Addressing

One of the biggest improvements in the Notes 8 client is the manner in which type-ahead mail addressing works. There is now a "type down" feature. As you type in an address, names that match the characters appear in a drop-down list. This allows you to address emails quickly. The names that appear are in the order of frequency of use rather than alphabetically. If you have a contact that you frequently mail, this user will appear at the top of the list and can be brought up with minimal key-strokes. Clicking on the name in the list will add that name to the address field.

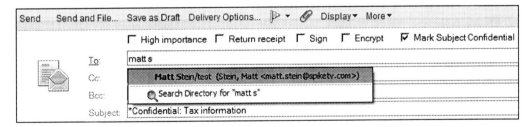

Multilevel Undo

The multilevel undo functionality for text editing in Notes 8 is now up to 50 levels. This applies to any text field in Notes 8, not just email text fields.

Inline Spell Checking

Inline spell checking can now be enabled. When this is enabled, a red squiggle will appear underneath any misspelled word (or more precisely a word that does not appear in the dictionary) in a rich-text field. This option can be enabled in the unified preferences.

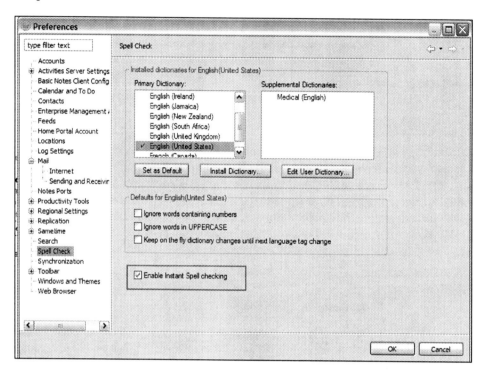

Right-clicking the word with the red squiggle displays a list of suggested spellings. Clicking on one of the suggested spellings will replace a misspelled word with this word. You can also add the word to the dictionary. This will prevent the word from being marked as misspelled in the future.

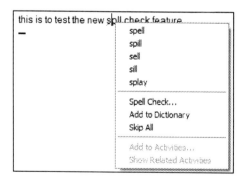

When inline spell checking is enabled, it is available in any Notes document.

Document Selection

Lotus Notes 8 has changed the way in which documents are selected. In previous Notes releases, a check mark was placed next to a document's name. Notes 8 now supports common operating system commands and mouse clicks. To select multiple documents, hold down the *Shift* key and select the documents. To select an individual document, hold down the *Control* key and click on the document. This will highlight the selected documents and allow you to work with them in a group.

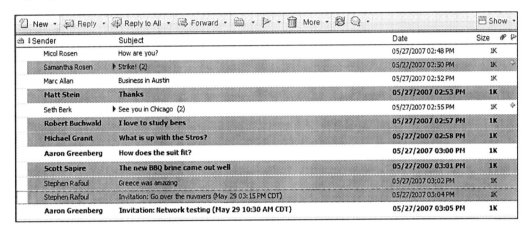

Common operating system commands and mouse clicks work in the calendar and contact views as well.

Recent Collaborations

Have you ever wanted to view your conversations with a specific person, from multiple tools such as instant messaging, email, activities, and calendaring? Notes 8 contains a right-click option that will allow you to view all your dealings with that person. A window titled **Recent Collaborations** will display a list from which you can select and open any recent collaboration.

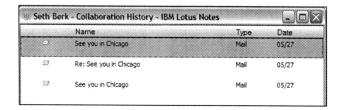

The right-click option to view recent collaborations will work in the calendar and contact views as well.

Message Recall

Sometimes users accidentally send a message before finishing it, or send it to unintended recipients. Message recall can now help you in these sticky situations. To recall the message, just select it in your **Sent** view and click on the **Recall Message** button.

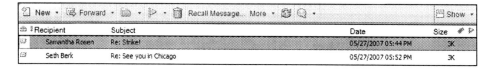

After you click the **Recall Message** button, a dialog box will appear with options. You can select which recipients from who to recall the message. You also have the option to recall a message even if it was already read.

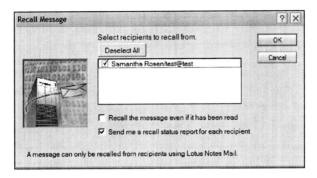

If you would like to receive a recall status report, check the **Send me a recall status report for each recipient** option. This will send you a status report.

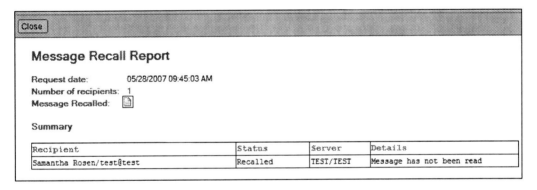

You will only be able to use this feature from the **Sent** view of your mail file. The sent message must be available for the information about the recipients to be used to recall the message. If the message was not saved when sent, you cannot recall it.

 Message recall will only work if the user is on Lotus Domino 8 server and the feature is enabled. The user must also be configured for use in a mail policy.

Improved "Out of Office" Functionality

The "Out of Office" functionality has been enhanced on the Notes client, as well as on the server. This section will cover these enhancements. The settings are now more granular, allowing you to set the hour that you are leaving and returning. You can also choose to only have the "Out of Office" message sent in reply to the first message that someone sends or in reply to all messages that they sends.

Manually disabling the "Out of Office" feature is a thing of the past. The feature disables itself when the "Out of Office" time expires. This saves time by requiring less administrative tasks upon your return. A person who is delegated to your calendar cannot enable and disable the Out of Office for you.

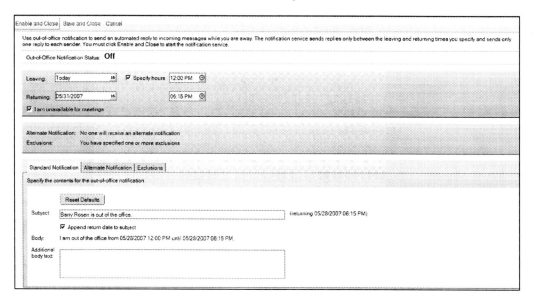

New Calendar Functionality

The **Calendar** view has been updated in Lotus Notes 8. The following sections cover the new features in the calendar.

View Navigation

To keep the view navigation consistent, the calendar can be navigated from the view navigator pane on the left-hand side of the Notes 8 interface.

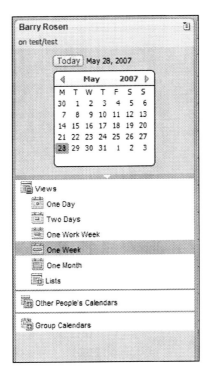

Action Bar

As in the mail view, the action bar is designed to offer single click functionality. More options can be accessed with the **Respond** button.

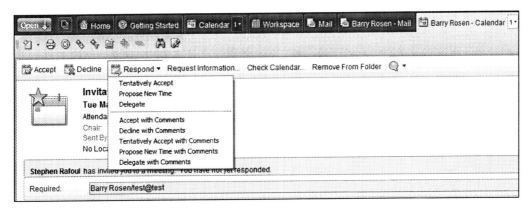

Display of All-Day Events

Now all-day events are displayed for the entire day. To save you the bother of scrolling up, the title of the all-day event will appear at the top of the page regardless of what time of the day you are viewing in the calendar. Anniversaries behave in the same manner as all-day events.

Manage New Invitations from Your Calendar View

A new feature in Notes 8 is the ability to display unprocessed events on your calendar, next to processed events. (Unprocessed events are calendar events that have been received, but not yet accepted.) This allows you to see your calendar with all events before deciding to accept or decline.

By default, this feature is not enabled. You must enable this feature in your calendar preferences.

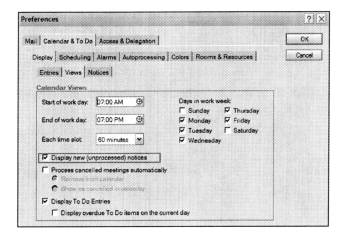

When enabled, your unprocessed items will appear in a color different from accepted items. They will appear in white with an envelope icon in the upper right-hand corner. Accepted invitations appear in blue with a person icon in the upper right-hand corner.

Show Cancelled Invitations in Your Calendar

Now you can choose to keep canceled invitations in your calendar. (In previous releases, you could auto-process cancellations so as to have them removed from your calendar.) The benefit of this new functionality is to keep a record of the cancelled meeting in your calendar, rather than just a cancellation notice in your inbox.

This is enabled in your calendar preferences.

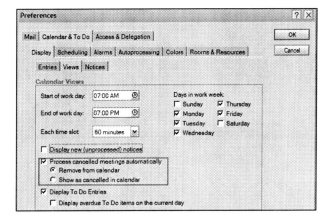

A cancelled meeting will be displayed in brown on your calendar without an icon. When you open the meeting from your calendar, it will be removed from this view.

Check Schedule

You can now check your schedule when you are creating a new meeting by clicking the **Check Schedule** button. This will bring up a window with the day view showing how the new meeting will fit into the schedule. (An alternative method to check your schedule is to use the side bar.)

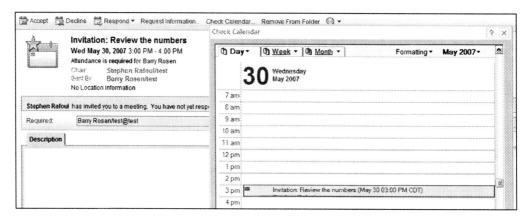

Locate Free Time for a Subset of Invitees

When inviting a large number of people to a meeting, it is often difficult to determine when all everyone will be available. Now you can select certain invitees and get free time information for them. For example, you can search only the required attendees.

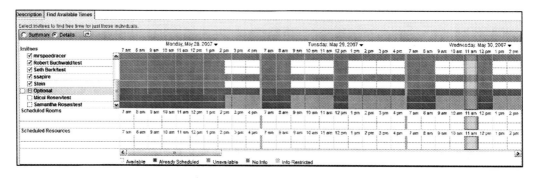

Contacts

In Notes 8, the `Contacts` user interface has been changed significantly. In particular, new features have been introduced. The `names.nsf` file that contains all local contacts has been renamed to `Contacts`. The following sections will describe the new interface and features.

Contact Form

The newly renamed `Contacts` database has additional forms which add flexibility to how you store your contacts.

There are more fields available when filling out the **Contact** form. You can see these new fields when placing a contact form in edit mode.

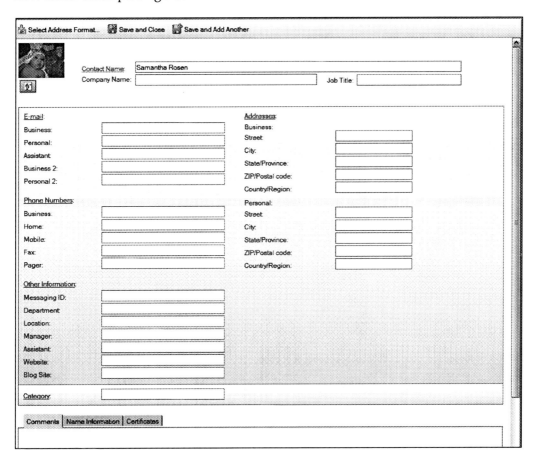

If the field is not filled in, it will not be displayed when viewing the saved contact.

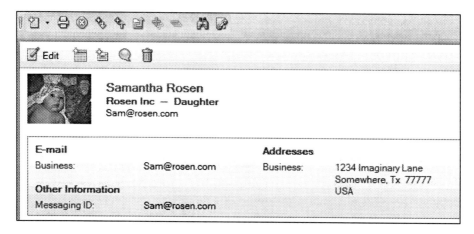

There are several formats in which the contact can be displayed, and you can choose which format is most appropriate.

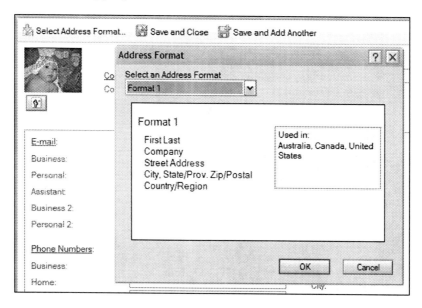

To make the forms more customizable, you can now change the titles of the fields to reflect your individual needs.

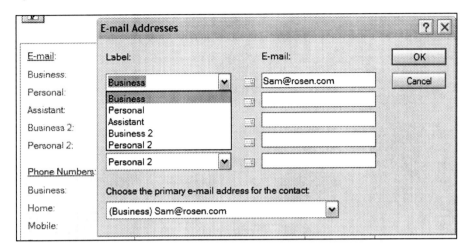

You can now store a photograph of your contact in the record by clicking on the **Insert Contact Photo** button in the top left corner of the **Contact** form.

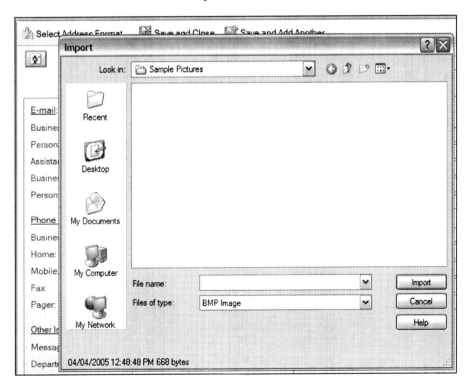

Business Card View

A new view, called **Business Card**, has been added to the `Contacts` database. This displays all your contacts in a business card format, making it easier to find contacts at a glance. To open the contact from this view, simply double-click it.

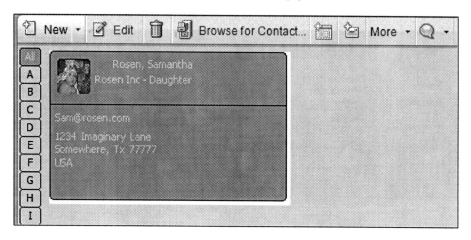

Recent Contacts

Another new view in the **Contacts** database is the **Recent Contacts** view. This view will display all of the people with whom you have recently collaborated. This makes it easier for you to address frequently used contacts. It is from this view that the client gets the addresses that populate the pull-down menu that appears when you send a memo or an invititation. This allows you to pull up any email address that you have sent messages to you. You can also pull up any addresses you have been copied on, and add them to an email that you are addressing.

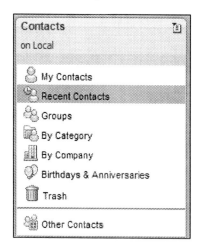

From the **Replication** page you can choose to have your contacts synchronized. This will check for changes such as phone number or address changes from the server directory and synchronize them with your local **Contacts** database.

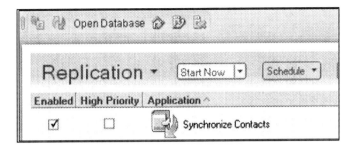

Summary

In this chapter, we have reviewed the major new features offered by the Lotus Notes 8 client. Many of these involve enhancements to the client user interface itself. Other new features include enhancements to mail, calendar, and contacts. These features significantly broaden the power and usefulness of the Notes client, while providing greater ease of use (and potentially minimal retraining) – an important consideration for any user planning to upgrade to Notes 8.

3

Lotus Notes 8 and SOA

In this chapter, we will introduce the concept of a service oriented architecture (SOAs) and how Lotus Notes 8 fits into one. We will explain what an SOA is, its value, and its characteristics. You will also learn how Lotus Notes 8 has many of the characteristics of SOA components, and how it can help you assemble applications that can play a role in an SOA. (However, this chapter is not intended to provide the in-depth detail necessary to implement your own SOA.)

What is an SOA?

Although the concept of an SOA is simple, the components that make up one can be complex. Additionally, the value and perception of an SOA varies with the perspective and role of organizations and persons considering one. So in this chapter, we'll start with the basic definition of an SOA and then examine specific aspects of SOAs.

"SOA" stands for *service oriented architecture*. This definition can often be taken further by adding the word "business", since the inherent value of an SOA comes from business orientation and enablement.

In computing, the term SOA expresses a software architectural concept that defines the use of services to support the requirements of software users. In an SOA environment, nodes on a network make resources available to other participants in the network as independent services they access in a standardized way. Most definitions of an SOA identify the use of web services (using SOAP and WSDL) in its implementation. However, you can implement SOA using any service-based technology.

SOAs can be used to:

- Build distributed systems that deliver application functionality as services to either end-user applications or other users.

- Design and implement distributed systems that allow a tight correlation between the business model and its IT implementation.

- Manage services made available by different software packages for reuse and reconfiguration.

These uses of SOA highlight the fact that they encompasses a wide range of interests.

There are many ways to implement and view an SOA. The specific approach and value proposition depends on the needs of the business and the role of the organization or person considering the SOA. In this chapter, we will focus on how business how to reuse existing Notes-based functions, and how to take existing Eclipse and WebSphere Portal services and incorporate them into new Notes functions.

The Characteristics of an SOA

There are some commonly understood characteristics of an SOA. These include the following:

- Services are reusable and called by many applications.

- Service access is with communication protocols rather than direct calls.

- Services are loosely coupled so that they are autonomous.

- Interfaces are defined in a platform-independent manner.

- Services are encapsulated so that the interface doesn't reveal how the service was implemented. (This is called abstraction.)

- Services share a formal contract.

- Services are composable (able to be assembled into composite applications).

- Services are stateless.

- Services are discoverable.

Later in this chapter, we will examine some of these characteristics and see how Lotus Notes 8 can interact with an SOA.

Perspectives on SOAs

From a business perspective, SOA is about identifying, surfacing, and integrating business services to meet business needs.

From an IT perspective, SOA is about responding quickly to changing business needs. IT organizations must determine what style, patterns, or principles provide architecture capable of responding in a timely fashion. These questions must be answered with the understanding that existing applications and systems have been built over time and are hard-wired together.

Why SOAs Now?

One key factor in the emergence and success of SOAs is the evolution of standards. Standardization has made SOAs more useful now than ever before. In the past, companies have made numerous attempts to develop a standard to support some version of SOAs. Standards such as CORBA and DCOM have existed for a while, but haven not been sufficiently widely adopted to allow true interconnection of companies and people.

Thanks to the Internet and standards such as HTML and HTTP, companies and customers are linked together as never before. This linkage is the key to the interconnection and combination of services that distinguish an SOA. As the Internet has matured, web services standards have emerged; they now have a common set of standards across vendors and businesses. Major vendors have agreed on standardization of web services and have incorporated these standardized services into products, providing unprecedented breadth of tools for supporting an SOA. Standards for interoperability that have been widely adopted include:

- HTTP
- XML
- SOAP
- WSDL
- UDDI
- OASIS standards such as ODF

Other factors play key roles in the adoption of SOAs. For example, mature software and software frameworks are now available across a breadth of vendors, including Eclipse and OSGi. SOA-related governance models and best practices are defined and proven. With the development of the Internet, implementation is now practical, and business/IT collaboration is receiving renewed focus.

SOA Lifecycle

There are four distinct phases to the lifecycle of an SOA: model, assemble, deploy, and manage.

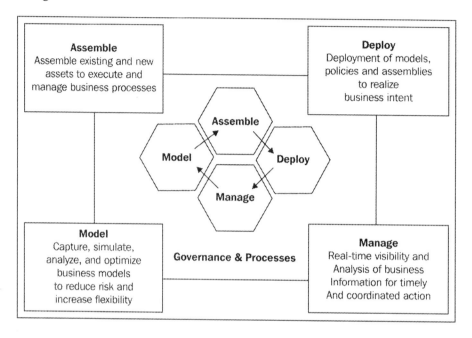

This lifecycle provides a framework within which an SOA can be built. However, businesses and IT organizations can choose where within the lifecycle to begin an SOA implementation. (One of the key values of SOA is the ability to get quick benefits by assembling and deploying services without waiting for a full-blown SOA definition.)

The Model Phase

The model phase of the SOA lifecycle starts with discovering which program assets can be reuse in new applications. You can discover these hidden assets and determine which programs are good candidates for reuse in web applications with a number of tools already on the market.

As we stated earlier, the key value of an SOA is the surfacing of business services. So as to properly identify the business services and understand how they fit into the business, SOA modelling uses establishes a common understanding of the business processes, objectives, and outcomes between business and IT. The SOA model helps make sure that any IT applications meet the needs of the business and provide a baseline for business service performance.

At the end of the model phase, you should have a clear inventory of assets showing where they can be used in the business processes that you have modelled.

The Assemble Phase

The assemble phase is where programs are wrapped as services and used to create composite applications which bring together core assets that often span multiple platforms. If you use legacy host transactional environments, the tools simplify the development of new web user interfaces, traditional terminal interfaces, and back-end business logic.

During the assemble phase, you can create services out of existing assets such as ERP and financial systems, legacy host applications, and other solutions that are currently running your business. If no functionality exists, you can create and test a service to deliver the functionality required for your business process. Once the required services are available, you can orchestrate them so as to implement your business process.

Lotus Notes 8 includes features to support the assemble phase of SOA development. We will review those capabilities later in this chapter.

The Deploy Phase

During the deploy phase, you can configure and scale the runtime environment to meet the service levels required by your business process. You can optimize the services environment to reliably run mission-critical business processes while providing the flexibility to make updates dynamically in response to changing business requirements.

Once it is configured, you can deploy your business process into a robust, scalable, and secure services environment. This service-oriented approach can reduce the cost and complexity associated with maintaining numerous point-to-point integrations.

The Manage Phase

The manage phase involves managing the underlying service assets, establishing and maintaining service availability and response times, and managing and maintaining version control over the services that make up your business processes. The management phase ultimately enables you to make better business decisions sooner than previously possible.

You can monitor key performance indicators in real time to get the information required to prevent, isolate, diagnose, and fix problems, enabling you to provide feedback into the business process model so as to enable continuous improvement.

Once the SOA has been deployed, you'll need to continue to secure, manage, and monitor the composite applications and underlying resources from both an IT and a business perspective so as to get full value from the SOA. Information gathered during the manage phase on key SOA indicators can provide real-time insight into business processes, enabling you to make better business decisions, and feeding information back into the SOA lifecycle for continuous process improvement.

How Lotus Notes 8 Works with SOAs

Now that we've covered the basics of an SOA, it is time to examine how Lotus Notes 8 fits in. Lotus Notes 8 can help an organization achieve an architecture with SOA characteristics by:

- Supporting service reuse. Lotus Notes 8 does this by providing a composite application development capability, and by providing web service consumer and producer capability.

- Enabling further extension of Lotus Notes to further work with SOAs through an open technologies framework

Composite Applications

Lotus Notes 8 has the ability to assemble composite applications. This ability is useful in the assemble phase of the SOA lifecycle. In this section, you will learn what a composite application is and how Lotus Notes 8 enables the assembly of composite applications.

A composite application is a loosely coupled collection of user-facing components brought together for a specific business purpose. Composite applications provide the front end of an SOA. The ability to create and edit composite applications lets you easily combine and reuse different services, providing a tremendous platform for service reuse – a key characteristic of an SOA. With Lotus Notes 8, server-managed, NSF-based composite applications can be created or edited. An NSF-based composite application can consist of NSF, Eclipse, and WebSphere Portal components.

Elimination of information and service "silos" is a key benefit of composite applications for end users. With composite applications, the services are loosely coupled and independent (not hard-wired into the infrastructure) so they can be easily reused or extended, as business needs change. This is an important element in enabling a business to flexibly respond to business changes and to alter application interactions as needs dictate. Available online or offline, composite applications can facilitate self-service activities. Using the composite application editor within Lotus Notes 8 software, end users and LOB managers can create composite applications. IT staff can use their current development skills to build and modify reusable components, helping to reduce IT and development costs. Organizations can reuse previously developed Eclipse technology-based components within the composite applications experienced by Lotus Notes and Domino 8 software, helping to increase return on investment in application development tools and skills.

The composite application editor is an install-time option of the Lotus Notes 8 Client. Composite applications can be built with minimal or no NSF design changes to reuse existing Notes applications as components of the composite application.

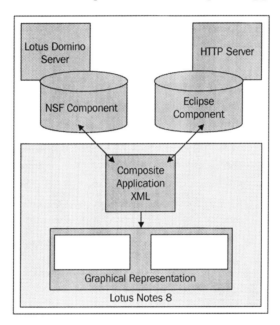

Development responsibilities for building composite applications can be distributed across several types of application development and administration team members. The process does not have to be restricted to a highly skilled component developer. The roles in composite application development typically include the following:

- A component developer who designs and creates NSF and Eclipse components.

- An application assembler who defines and assembles the composite application, and who may be business user.

- An application administrator who deploys portlets onto the WebSphere portal and maintains NSF-based composite applications on the Domino server.

The following section provides an example of how Lotus Notes 8 enables composite-application assembly. The documentation and files necessary to build this example can be found at: `http://www-03.ibm.com/developerworks/blogs/page/CompApps?entry=more_sophisticated_tutorial_of_composite`

You can also find a blog discussing composite applications in Lotus Notes 8 at: `http://www-03.ibm.com/developerworks/blogs/page/CompApps`

This example involves three components:

- Lotus Notes Contacts
- A Notes Domino forum application
- An Eclipse component implementing a Tag Cloud

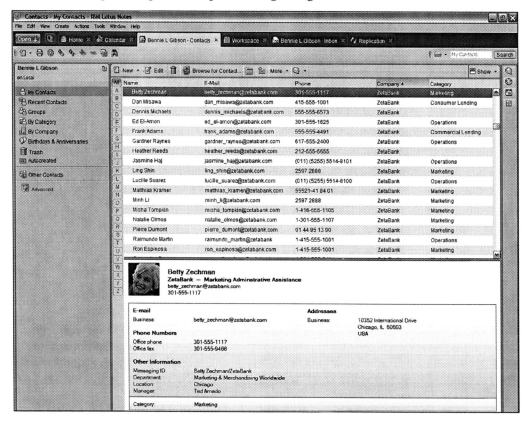

The above figure shows the Lotus Notes **Contacts** view. On its own, this component shows a list of contacts and has a preview pane showing the details for the currently selected contact. Certainly, this is a valuable service by itself. But our example shows how you can reuse this service, combine it with other services, and extend the value of this component.

The second component of this example is a Lotus Notes discussion application. This component allows users to discuss topics (in this case, Lotus Notes Designer) in a user discussion forum setting. Again, this on its own is a useful component, but our example will combine this component with the Lotus Notes Contacts to create a new, more useful service by loosely coupling these components.

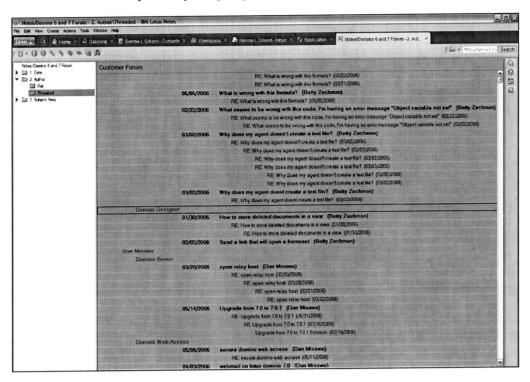

In the first step in this example, the Lotus Notes 8 Designer is uses WSDL (Web Services Description Language) to expose properties and actions needed to navigate within the Notes Forum application. Below is one screen from the Lotus Notes 8 Designer where the final step of the WSDL creation is being completed.

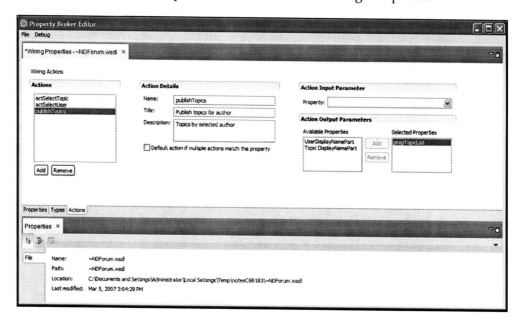

In addition to using WSDL, Lotus Notes 8 Designer also allows you to create actions to be implemented during assembly of a composite application. In this case, the action is called **Select Person**.

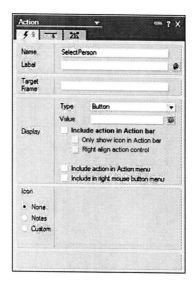

This action will select the forum entry for the current selection in the Lotus Notes Contacts component.

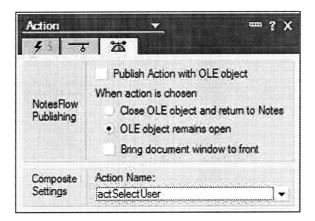

With the appropriate WSDL action associated with the Notes Forum application, the prerequisites for assembling the composite application are in place. In the following figure, the composite application editor is used to wire the Notes **Contact** view and the Notes Forum application.

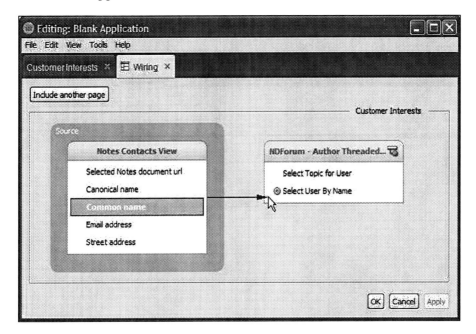

The result is a composite application in which the Notes Forum entry is displayed based on the selected Notes contact entry. As you can see in the following figure, Betty Zachman of ZetaBank is the currently selected Lotus Notes contact and the Lotus Notes forum has been advanced to show the threads for Betty Zachman.

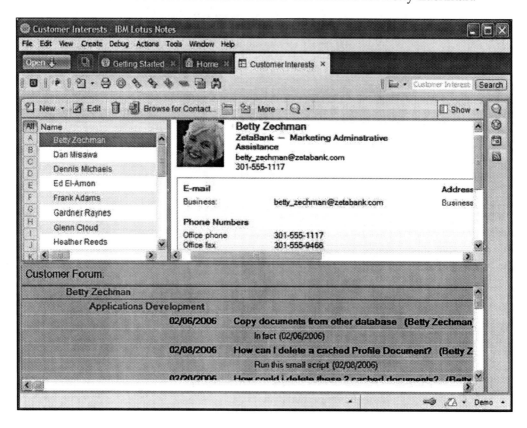

Next, the composite application editor is used to include an Eclipse tag cloud in the composite application. This component displays tag data about the current contact. This is accomplished by linking the Eclipse component to the Notes Forum application.

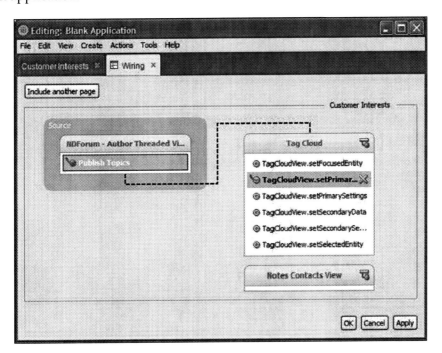

In this final figure, the current Lotus Notes contact selection is Betty Zachman and the interest selected is application development. The result is a view of the Notes forum positioned in a thread by Betty Zachman related to application development.

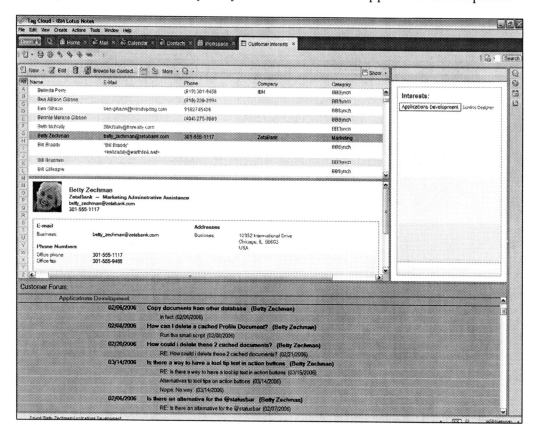

This simple example shows the power of the Lotus Notes 8 composite application editor. Minimal Lotus Notes designer effort, combined with use of the Lotus Notes 8 Client composite application editor, can produce a new business function reusing existing heterogeneous services.

Lotus Notes 8 and Web Services

Web services producer and consumer capability is not new to Lotus Notes 8. However, the ability to produce and consume web services is a key characteristic of an SOA. This section provides an overview of how Lotus Notes supports web service production and consumption.

A web service provider makes available a WSDL (Web Services Description Language) document that defines the service interface. The WSDL document is in XML format. What happens behind the interface is up to the provider, but most providers map the interface to procedure calls in a supported programming language. Incoming requests from a consumer are passed to the underlying code, and results are passed back to the consumer.

Lotus Domino maps the WSDL interface to an agent-like web service design element that can be coded in LotusScript or Java. The web service must be on a Domino server with HTTP enabled. (We can test the web service through an HTTP session in the Notes client preview.) Access is through one of the following Domino URL commands:

- **OpenWebService** invokes the web service in response to a SOAP-encoded message sent through an HTTP POST request. An HTTP GET request (for example, a browser query) returns the name of the service and its operations.
- **WSDL** returns the WSDL document in response to an HTTP GET.

Several approaches can be used to create a web service design element in Domino Designer. One approach is to code the service entirely in LotusScript or Java. In this case, saving the design element generates a WSDL document that reflects the LotusScript or Java code. Alternatively, an existing WSDL document can be imported. In this case, the LotusScript or Java code reflects the operations in the imported WSDL document. The web service design element saves the WSDL document as well as the code. If the public interface has not changed, the WSDL document stays as it is. If anything in the coding that affects the public interface is changed, a new WSDL document is generated.

In Domino Designer, the web service design element resides below **Agents** under **Shared code**.

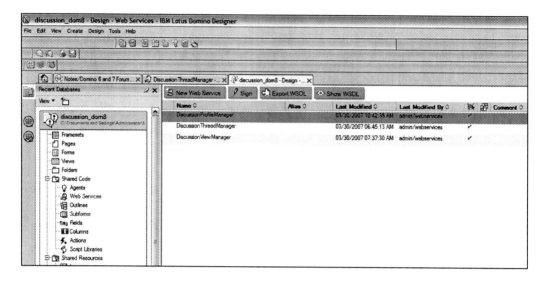

The web service design window looks a lot like the agent design window. Clicking the **New Web Service** button creates a new web service. Double-clicking the name of an existing web service opens it for editing.

An example of a web service to access Domino databases can be found here:

```
http://www-10.lotus.com/ldd/sandbox.nsf/ByDate/
7b12bb2e3f4a78be852572c3005bac80?OpenDocument
```

Lotus Notes 8 and Open Technologies

Lotus Notes 8 supports both OASIS/ODF and Eclipse open formats.

OASIS/ODF

Lotus Notes 8 supports both OASIS/ODF and Eclipse open formats.
Word-processing, spreadsheet, and presentation applications are basic, standard tools that many business users need and use on a daily basis. Lotus Notes 8 includes a suite of office productivity tools that allow end users to create, edit, and collaborate on a wide variety of file types. Lotus Notes 8 is packaged with IBM productivity tools that support the OASIS Open Document Format (ODF). ODF is an international standard for saving and sharing editable documents, such as word-processing documents, spreadsheets and presentations.

Eclipse

At the core of Lotus Notes 8 software is IBM's version of Eclipse Rich Client Platform (RCP) technology, which introduces a new open-standards-based SOA that makes Lotus Notes 8 software more extensible. In fact, a number of the new features of Lotus Notes 8 are a direct result of this extensibility (for instance, Sametime integration and RSS feed integration).

IBM has built a common client platform named Lotus Expeditor (previously called WebSphere Everyplace Deployment or WED) that packages the Eclipse rich client platform with some extra services (security, synchronization, data, deployment, and more) that can be used across the IBM software product set. The Lotus Notes 8 client is a consumer of this Lotus Expeditor common platform. This provides additional functionality while ensuring "forward compatibility" for existing Lotus Notes and Domino applications.

Lotus Notes 8 software supports nearly all custom Lotus Notes applications built for prior versions and incorporates the open standards of the Eclipse application development framework, allowing the use of a componentized SOA. This provides helps to make it easy to aggregate, access, and deploy functionality from a mix of software programs and systems. It enables developers to build applications more quickly and to reuse existing assets as business needs evolve.

Summary

In this chapter, we introduced service oriented architectures (SOAs) and saw how Lotus Notes 8 supports it. We then looked at several Notes 8 features and capabilities that can help you implement SOA-based architectures within your own organization.

We saw that, with a foundation in open technologies like Eclipse and with the introduction of the composite application editor, Lotus Notes 8 can be a key part of an SOA.

We also saw that currently Lotus Notes 8 only participates directly in the assemble phase of an SOA lifecycle. However, the open framework on which Lotus Notes 8 is based provides a highly flexible platform, and we can expect to see significant growth of Lotus Notes as a key factor in the growth and adoption of SOAs.

4
Productivity Tools

With the Lotus Notes 8 client comes a new suite of productivity tools which support the OASIS Open Document Format (ODF). ODF is an international standard that provides support for multiple file formats for word processing, presentations, and spreadsheets. By adopting this format, IBM has allowed Notes users to read and save documents in the Microsoft Office format as well as read from IBM Lotus SmartSuite documents. Both can be saved as ODF documents or as PDF format documents.

The advantage of using the productivity tools with ODF is that you no longer have to purchase an application from a single vendor in order to share and save your documents. Using a non commercial ODF product, will allow you to avoid having to maintain licenses, and also allow you to stop worrying about your software reaching the end of its shelf life. These benefits can lead to a lower TCO for maintaining software for document-based data.

This chapter provides an overview of the three productivity tools that are provided with the client:

- IBM Lotus Documents
- IBM Lotus Presentations
- IBM Lotus Spreadsheets

These productivity tools are also referred to as document editors, since you use them to create and edit documents in various formats (word processing, presentations, and spreadsheets respectively).

Productivity Tools Integration with Notes 8

The Eclipse architecture of the Notes 8 client supports the integration of other applications. One key example of this is the integration of the productivity tools. The preferences for the tools are in the `Preferences` interface. When opening the preference options for the productivity tools, you will see the following:

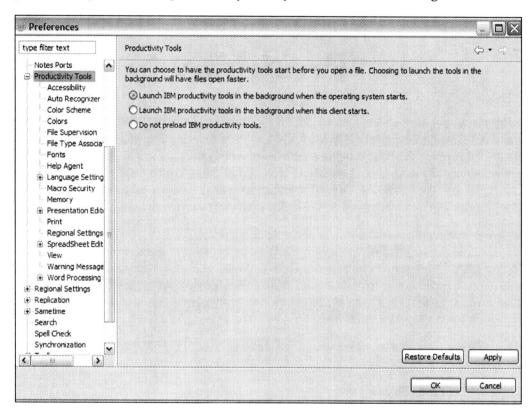

This setting will load a file called `soffice.exe`. This file corresponds to a stub that remains resident so that the tools will launch more quickly. If you do not want this to occur, choose the setting not to pre-load the productivity tools.

The productivity tools are independent of the Domino 8 server. This means that the tools will function without a Lotus Domino 8 server. They can even be launched when the Notes client is not running. To do this, either double-click on the icon on your desktop, or select the program from the **Start** menu.

Productivity Tools and Domino Policies

A Domino administrator can control the productivity tools through a **Productivity Tools** policy setting. This gives the administrator the ability to control who can use the tools (and also control whether or not macros are permitted to run). It will also control what document types will be opened by the productivity tools.

Productivity Tools Settings

Basics | Comments | Administration

Basics

Name:

Description:

Productivity Tools		How to apply this setting:	Inherit from parent policy:	Enforce in child policies:
Allow users to run macros in IBM productivity tools:	☐ Yes	Don't set value	☐ Inherit	☐ Enforce
Allow IBM productivity tools:	☐ Yes	Don't set value	☐ Inherit	☐ Enforce
Open MS Office files with IBM productivity tools:	☐ Yes	Don't set value	☐ Inherit	☐ Enforce
.doc	☐ Yes	Don't set value	☐ Inherit	☐ Enforce
.ppt	☐ Yes	Don't set value	☐ Inherit	☐ Enforce
.xls	☐ Yes	Don't set value	☐ Inherit	☐ Enforce
.rtf	☐ Yes	Don't set value	☐ Inherit	☐ Enforce
Open MS Office templates with IBM productivity tools:	☐ Yes	Don't set value	☐ Inherit	☐ Enforce
.dot	☐ Yes	Don't set value	☐ Inherit	☐ Enforce
.pot	☐ Yes	Don't set value	☐ Inherit	☐ Enforce
.xlt	☐ Yes	Don't set value	☐ Inherit	☐ Enforce
Open SmartSuite files with IBM productivity tools:	☐ Yes	Don't set value	☐ Inherit	☐ Enforce
.lw3	☐ Yes	Don't set value	☐ Inherit	☐ Enforce
.123	☐ Yes	Don't set value	☐ Inherit	☐ Enforce
.prz	☐ Yes	Don't set value	☐ Inherit	☐ Enforce
Open SmartSuite templates with IBM productivity tools:	☐ Yes	Don't set value	☐ Inherit	☐ Enforce
.mwp	☐ Yes	Don't set value	☐ Inherit	☐ Enforce
.12m	☐ Yes	Don't set value	☐ Inherit	☐ Enforce
.mas	☐ Yes	Don't set value	☐ Inherit	☐ Enforce
.smc	☐ Yes	Don't set value	☐ Inherit	☐ Enforce

IBM Lotus Documents

The IBM Lotus Documents productivity tool is a document editor that allows you to create documents containing graphics, charts, and tables. You can save your documents in multiple formats. IBM Lotus Documents has a spell checker, which provides for instant corrections, and many other tools that can be used to enhance documents. No matter what the complexity of the documents that you are creating or editing, this productivity tool can handle the job.

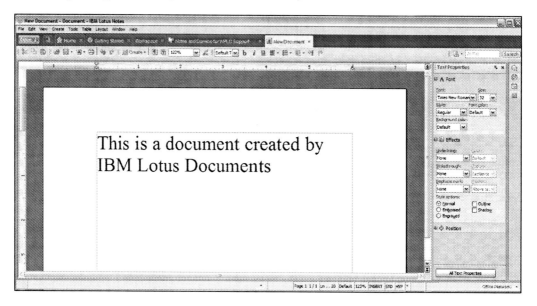

IBM Lotus Presentations

The IBM Lotus Presentations tool will allow you to create professional presentations featuring multimedia, charts, and graphics. The presentations tool comes with templates that you can use to create your slide shows. If you wish, you can create and save your own templates as well. The templates that you create should be saved to the following directory: \Notes\framework\shared\eclipse\plugins\com. ibm.productivity.tools.template.en_3.0.0.20070428-1644\layout. (You can save a template in a different directory, but you'll need to navigate to it when creating a new presentation from that template.)

Not only can you apply dynamic effects to the presentations, but you can also publish them in a variety of formats.

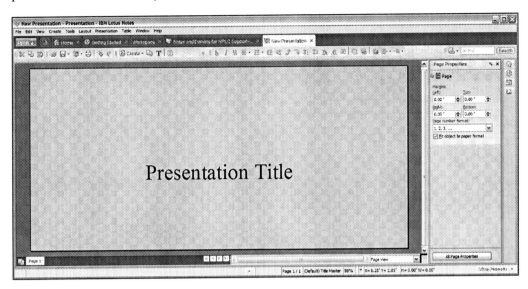

IBM Lotus Spreadsheets

As its name indicates, IBM Lotus Spreadsheets is a tool used to create spreadsheets. You can use this tool to calculate, display, and analyze your data. As with other spreadsheet applications, the tool allows you to use functions to create formulas that perform advanced calculations with your data.

One feature gives you the ability to change one factor in a calculation with many factors so that the user can see how it effects the calculation. This is useful when exploring multiple scenarios. IBM Lotus Spreadsheets also has a dynamic function that will automatically update charts when the data changes.

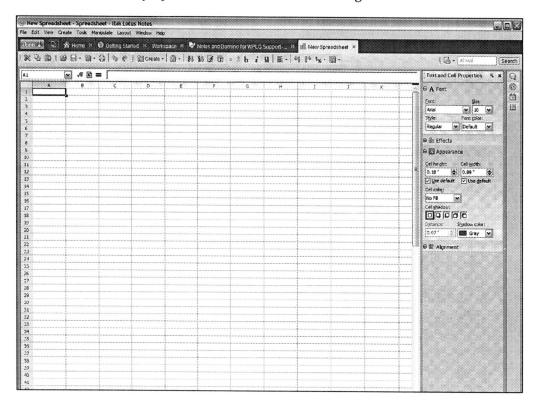

Summary

In this chapter, we have reviewed the productivity tools provided with the Notes 8 client. These tools include IBM Lotus Documents, IBM Lotus Presentations, and IBM Lotus Spreadsheets. We have briefly examined how these tools are integrated with Notes 8, and how they are controlled by Domino policy documents.

5
Lotus Domino 8 Server Features

As you can see from Chapter 2 of this book, a major focus of development activities for release 8 is the Lotus Notes client. However, there are a number of significant improvements and new features added to the Domino 8 server. These include mail-related features such as message recall and immediate notification of "Out of Office" status. Other core components have been enhanced, such as cluster replication, Domino Domain Monitoring, and security. Server performance has been improved, while maintaining backwards compatibility and ease of upgrade, which does not require changes to the hardware, the operating system, or even the On-Disk Structure (ODS).

This chapter reviews the new features and enhancements in Domino 8. We will discuss the following:

- End user and messaging enhancements such as mail recall and automated inbox cleanup.
- Administrator enhancements such as improved Domino Domain Monitoring.
- Performance enhancements such as streaming cluster replication and an improved AdminP process.
- Directory and security enhancements such as the integration of Directory Integrator and new directory views.
- Integration with other IBM technologies.

Our goal is to provide an overview of these topics so as to help you better understand the new and enhanced features within Domino 8.

End-User and Messaging Enhancements

There a number of new features provided to both end users and administrators in Lotus Domino 8. This section will focus on the following:

- Message recall
- "Out of Office" service
- Automated inbox cleanup
- Transfer and delivery delay reports
- Connection termination error limits

Message Recall

You can now recall mail messages that have been sent to other users within a Lotus Domino environment. Previously, administrators needed to manually delete a message that had been inadvertently sent. This process was painstaking and often did not fully provide the ability to recall messages. The new message recall feature will allow the end users to initiate the recall of messages and (as long as the message has been routed only through the NRPC protocol) the recipient's mail server will attempt to recall the message.

The message recall feature will only work for users using the Notes 8 mail template with servers running Domino 8. It will work across domains as long as the message was only routed via NRPC; messages that get sent over SMTP through the Internet will not be able to be recalled.

The message recall feature is enabled and configured for the entire Domino 8 environment through a server configuration document. This server configuration document allows administrators to configure the service to recall messages, depending on whether or not they have been read by the end user, or depending on the age of the message.

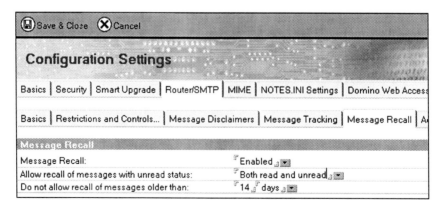

In addition to a global setting for the environment, message recall can be applied more granularly through the use of a mail policy. The mail policy can be configured to change the parameters for the end users, but the use of a policy does not override the global configuration. Within the policy document, administrators can set whether the end users can recall messages and whether messages sent to end users can be recalled. In addition, the policy can define whether or not to recall messages based on whether they have been read by the end user or have passed a predefined age.

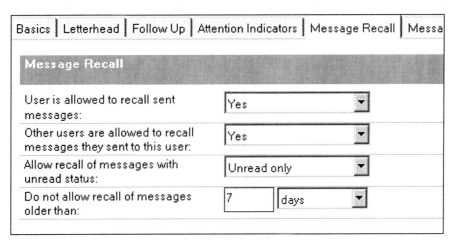

"Out of Office" Messages

In previous releases of Domino, "Out of Office" functionality was only offered as an agent. As a result, there was a delay in processing "Out of Office" messages for the end users. Typically, senders of messages to end users that had enabled their "Out of Office" agent would not receive notice for up to four hours based on the default configuration, but this could be greater based on internal implementations. Some environments were modified to inform senders of their "Out of Office" status at a more frequent interval. This shortening of the interval could affect the performance of the servers, because they would need to process the agent on a more frequent basis. The Domino 8 environment allows administrators to configure the "Out of Office" feature as a service on the server, rather than as an agent.

The configuration of the "Out of Office" feature as a service is not a requirement in Domino 8; the environment can continue to be configured via an agent. It is important to note that the utilization of Notes 8, the Notes 8 mail template, and a Domino 8 server is required for this feature to work. If the Notes 8 template or all servers (including cluster pairs) are not running Domino 8, you must configure the "Out of Office" feature as an agent.

Configuring the "Out of Office" feature as a service allows Domino 8 to send the "Out of Office" notification as soon as messages are received, after the server and end user mail rules are applied. Another enhancement of running the "Out of Office" feature as a service is that, once an end user enables the feature, upon the completion of the "Out of Office" time frame, the service is turned off after the first message is acted upon or through normal server maintenance routines.

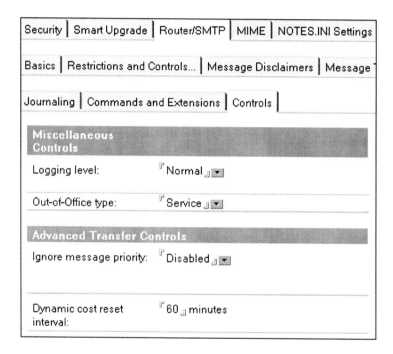

Enhanced Support for the Mail Thread Feature

Mail threads were introduced in early versions of Notes and Domino. The earlier implementation of mail threads within the inbox in Notes had some limitations, specifically when messages within the mail thread were deleted thus breaking the thread. Additionally, messages that were received from outside systems were not included in the mail thread. The Domino 8 support for client-based mail threads has been enhanced to ensure that the threads are persistent and that deletion or archiving of messages within the thread will not cause problems. In addition, enhanced support for messages outside of the Domino environment has been extended and can be included within the mail threads.

The enhanced mail features are delivered through the Domino server to the end user, therefore the Domino 8 mail thread functionality is not dependent on Notes 8 (since the Notes 7 client will provide the mail threads within the inbox view), the Notes 8 mail template, or the Domino 8 server for the senders or intermediate servers that will route the mail. The end user's mail server must be running Domino 8 for it to deliver the enhanced functionality.

Automated Inbox Cleanup

An excessive number of documents in a single view can be a significant end-user performance issue, particularly the primary view when the database is open. The number of documents in the Inbox view within the mail database can hinder performance by increasing the time required to build the view. When end users leave all of their incoming messages in the inbox view and do not archive messages or place them in folders, the inbox can become unwieldy. Domino 8 introduces the Automated Inbox cleanup process that removes messages from the inbox.

The Automated Inbox Cleanup feature can either be set through the server configuration document:

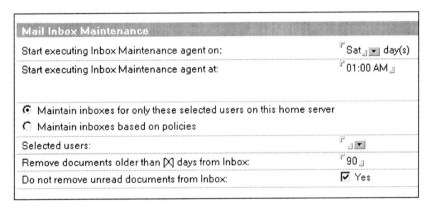

or through the use of a mail policy:

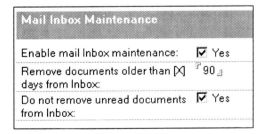

This feature doesn't require Notes 8 or the Notes 8 mail template, but your mail databases need to be hosted on a Domino 8 server. Through the server configuration document and the mail policy document, administrators can set the schedule for inbox maintenance based on the day and time.

Administrators can add this functionality for all users or a select group of users. The inbox cleanup can occur with a specified time frame and can leave documents in the inbox if they have not been read.

Reverse Path Setting for Forwarded Messages

As spam filters and other technologies proliferate, so has the use of reverse lookups for ensuring the proper address is used so that messages are not rejected. When a mail rule is set to forward messages within Domino 8 and the forwarded message contains a null value, some spam filters may reject the message. The new reverse path setting feature in Domino 8 allows for the setting of the path so as to ensure that messages are not rejected. Within the server configuration document, administrators have the ability to set the reverse path for forwarded mail.

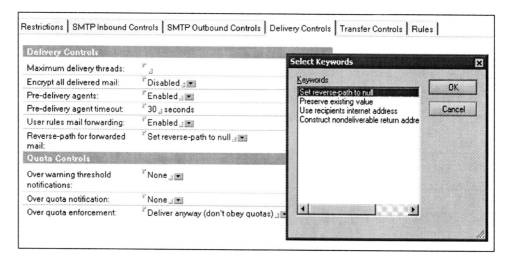

Rejecting Ambiguous Names Denying Mail to Groups

In some SMTP configurations, the environment is set up so as to conduct lookups to the directory before routing messages within the infrastructure. When this setting is configured, the server will reject ambiguous addresses for end users and groups.

Upon rejection of the message, a return message is routed to inform the sender that the message has been rejected by the Domino environment based on a corporate policy.

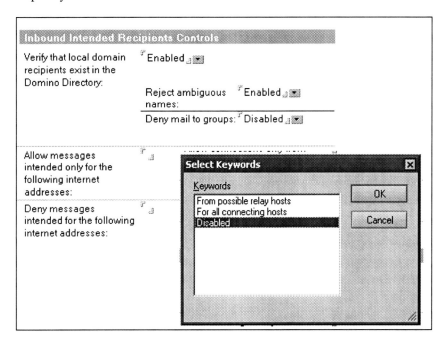

There are a number of other new and enhanced features in Domino 8 including router group expansion, transfer and delivery of delay reports, and improved HTML rendering for email. Refer to Domino 8 Administrator Help for more information on these and other topics.

Administration Enhancements

Domino administrators will welcome a number of important enhancements in Domino 8 including:

- Enhancements to the end user renaming process
- Enhancements to the AdminP process
- Enhancements to the Domino Domain Monitor (DDM) feature

The End User Renaming Process

The end user renaming process in Domino is executed by leveraging the AdminP process. When the request for a change in the user's name or shift in the hierarchy is submitted, the AdminP process begins to execute the renaming process in all databases throughout the environment. This ensures that ACLs, reader fields, and so on are updated with the new information. These requests are very intensive and (depending on the size and complexity of the environment) can take a considerable amount of time.

In Domino 8, the new names list feature builds a list of author and reader names found in the database, which the AdminP process can then use. If the name is found in the list, the AdminP process will make the appropriate changes to the fields. This new feature will increase the efficiency with which the AdminP process executes name changes throughout the environment. The limitation for the names list is 4K; if the list is larger, the AdminP process reverts to looking through the entire database to identify the fields where the name exists.

If your servers are running Domino 8 and have the new On-Disk Structure (ODS) applied (see the section on the new ODS structure later in this chapter), then the AdminP process will be able to use this new names list feature.

The AdminP Process

The Lotus Domino environment invokes the AdminP process for executing requests (user renaming, database moves and deletes, and so on) and uses the AdminP database, which is built from the AdminP.ntf template. A replica copy of the database is placed on every server. As AdminP requests are generated, they are recorded on the administration server and then pushed out via replication to the other Domino servers. The servers will then look up and execute the tasks as required.

In Domino 8, requests that are generated for a specific server will be directly placed on that server as long as there is connectivity between the servers. The implementation of placing requests directly on the executing server should speed up the processing of the requests, because the replication of the AdminP database is removed from the process (which can cause some delays due to scheduling issues). There is no dependency on Notes 8 or the Notes 8 template to deliver this functionality, but the source server must be upgraded to Domino 8.

This enhancement of the AdminP process is the default setting in Domino 8. To disable this feature, set the following in Notes.ini:

```
ADMINP_DONT_ATTEMPT_DIRECT_DEPOSIT=1
```

Domino Domain Monitoring (DDM)

Domino Domain Monitoring (DDM) was introduced in Domino 7. The goal of DDM is to reduce the administrative workload required to troubleshoot and manage issues in the Domino environment. Prior to the introduction of DDM, administrators had so as to review a number of sources to collect the appropriate information to conduct problem determination. Domino 8 includes several enhancements to DDM.

WebSphere Services Probe

Domino 8 includes the ability to monitor the Lotus Connections' (the Lotus Connections software is not bundled with Domino, this function only enhances the monitoring capabilities) Activities function, which is hosted on a WebSphere server. A new WebSphere Services probe has been introduced so as to give the Domino administrator the ability to monitor the connectivity status of the activities servers.

Basics	
Probe Type:	Server
Probe Subtype:	WebSphere Services
Probe Description:	Websphere Activities Probe
	This probe checks to make sure protocol requests are being processed for WebSphere services. It does so by connecting to the port and performing a minimal protocol specific conversation.
Target	
Which servers should run this probe?	MailServer/Servers/Comp
Specifics	
Severity	Warning (high)
Target WebSphere Server Name:	activities.competitive.com
Port Numbers:	80

LDAP Search Reporting

Domino provides a robust LDAP server built into its base server functionality. As more and more environments become dependent on the LDAP services provided by Domino, it is important to ensure that searches are completed with appropriate response times. The new LDAP Search Response probe allows you to monitor and track response times as they relate to LDAP searches.

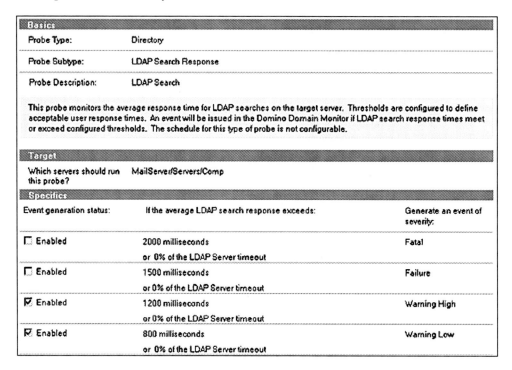

Common Actions Quick Access Feature

The DDM database within the Domino 8 environment provides a set of common tasks that are performed by administrators. From within the DDM database, you can simply click on the **Common Actions** drop-down menu and access routine administrative actions without switching to another view or client.

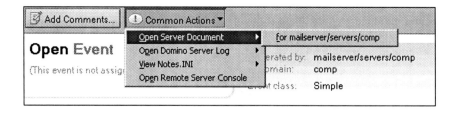

By Database View

Working through the DDM database can be difficult when you are trying to work on specific issues related to a single database. In Domino 7, administrators were required to search through the database or create a custom view and then maintain that view as new releases of the product were deployed. The new **By Database** view allows you to research specific issues related to a troublesome database or respond to a customer issue without having to ensure that the view is brought forward if it was customized in previous versions.

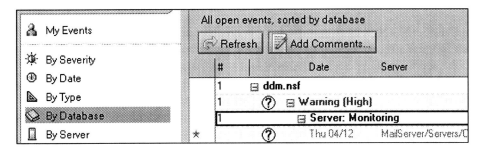

Other Domino 8 administration features include Domino Administrator integration with IBM CommonStore Archive Services, Web Administration Server Bookmarks, automatic report closing (administration probe subtype); execute CA role, modular documents, and others. For a more complete review of the DDM features, you should refer to the Domino 8 Administrator Help.

Performance Enhancements

Domino 8 includes a number of new features designed to enhance its performance. The focus of these enhancements is on reducing server overhead and load from functions within the environment.

This section will focus on the following new and enhanced features:

- Streaming cluster replication
- New ODS (design note compression, on-demand collations)
- Simple search controls

Streaming Replication

The cluster replication process moves information between the cluster member servers to ensure that, in case of a server outage, users maintain access to the most up-to-date information. As a new item is received on one server, the cluster replication process pushes the information to the other server. A typical configuration of the cluster replication task is to have one instance enabled on each server. You can increase the number of cluster replication tasks within the environment, but doing so increases disk I/O requirements, and this may have an effect on performance.

Domino 8 introduces a new feature for the cluster replication process, streaming replication. Streaming replication allows for the immediate transfer of information from one server to its cluster mate, without requiring the server to write to disk. The replication process occurs within the memory, thereby reducing I/O requirements. Cluster replications works closely with the normal replication process to ensure that the impact on the environment is reduced. Streaming replication is a server-based feature that does not require Notes 8 or the Notes 8 mail template.

New ODS

Domino 8 includes a new On-Disk Structure (ODS) that will allow the implementation of new features to increase performance and reduce the amount of overhead required to maintain and manage the environment. The new ODS 48 is not a requirement when moving to Domino 8. Instead, it is an option that takes advantage of the design note compression and on demand collation features. To upgrade the databases, add the line `Create_R8_Databases=1` to your server's `Notes.ini` file. To upgrade databases to the new ODS and compress the design, run a copy-style compaction. (The design note compression and view collation features require ODS 48.)

Design Note Compression

Design note compression is a new feature provided in Domino 8 to assist in reducing the space required by the database templates. The compression feature allows design elements to be compressed, thereby reducing disk requirements. Based on preliminary testing, database size could be reduced up to 55% to 60%. Design note compression does not require Notes 8 or the Notes 8 mail template, but since this is a server feature, the Domino 8 server is required.

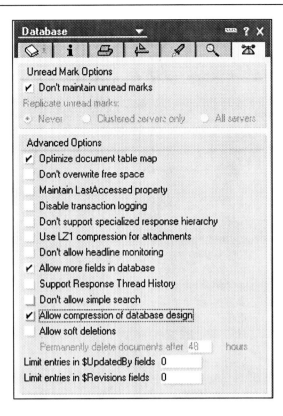

On-Demand Collation

A new Domino 8 feature is the ability to allow application developers to leave the creation of indexes until the end user leverages the sorting feature within the database. This option will reduce unnecessary overheads for the Domino server. To enable this feature, Notes 8 and the Notes 8 mail template are not required. But since this is a server-based feature, the Domino 8 server is required. To enable this feature, add the following line to `Notes.ini`: `ENABLE_ON_DEMAND_ COLLATIONS=1`.

Managing Simple Searches Effectively

The Notes/Domino environment allows for feature rich searching capabilities. These capabilities leverage the full text index created for a database. If a full text index has not been created when the user searches for the information, the server attempts to locate the information within the database. The process of searching the database without a full text index can significantly impact the performance of the server. In Domino 8, a new enhancement is introduced so as to eliminate the use of simple search and thus increase server performance.

By checking the **Don't Allow simple search** checkbox within the database properties tab, you can significantly enhance performance. If the database does not have a full text index and this feature is enabled, the end user will receive an error and the search will not be completed for the database.

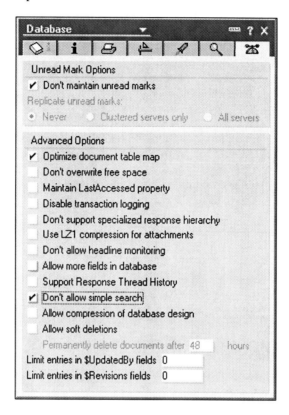

There are a number of other new performance-related features and enhancements in Domino 8. These include improved server availability in a cluster and critical request scheduling.

Domino Directory and Security Enhancements

Domino 8 offers a number of important Domino Directory and security enhancements. These include:

- IBM Tivoli Directory Integrator
- The Directory management tool

- Enhancements in Directory Assistance authentication
- Directory Assistance LDAP configuration wizards
- People view by Lotus Notes version
- Internet password lockout
- Enhanced ID recovery APIs
- Preventing access to Internet password fields
- Enhanced local database encryption
- Certificates

IBM Tivoli Directory Integrator

One of the most complicated problems to solve when implementing Domino (or any system that requires a directory to function) is locating the single authoritative source to use for access or identity management. Tivoli Director Integrator (TDI) is a directory integration engine that provides a system that allows business rules to be applied to synchronize data in any direction. TDI provides different "assembly lines" (integration components that use the TDI API to connect various stores so as to allow TDI to apply those business rules).

For example, if you have Microsoft Active Directory for file and print services, an LDAP store for web authentication, SAP or Peoplesoft for HR, or Lotus Domino, then TDI will allow granular control of user properties across all systems with TDI serving as the arbiter and synchronizing "master".

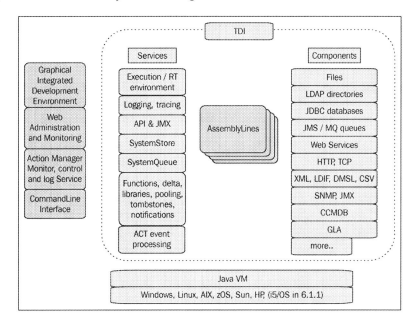

This applies to Domino as follows. With email, every message or calendar invitation that is sent requires a directory lookup to find the recipient for delivery. In typical organizations, the email directory and the authoritative directory are not the same. Domino 8 includes a license for TDI to synchronize these directories in a manner that previously has been extremely difficult and expensive.

The following illustration shows a connection from Microsoft Active Directory as the directory partner for Lotus Domino, where directory entries flow bi-directionally between the two systems.

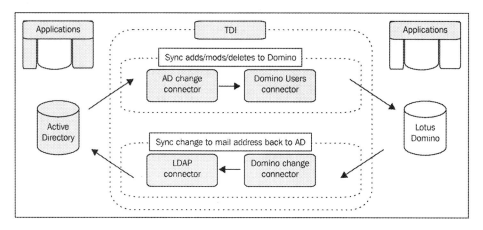

Previous versions of Domino included a tool known as ADSynch to perform a similar function. However, this tool was not as flexible or scalable as TDI. As the name suggests, ADSynch only synchronizes Active Directory and Domino. TDI can connect to nearly any system.

This model provides a single user interface for ID generation and management. If a user is created on either side, IDs and ancillary entries are created on the other. This could be with two systems as illustrated above, or with many systems and entries flowing to all the other systems user-specific attributes as defined by TDI.

When implementing Notes/Domino 8 in a "green field" environment or as a migration, the directory integration piece is a primary component, not just another feature to be added. With the addition of TDI, Notes/Domino 8 lets you bring in many different directories and provide services much more easily than before. However, this does not mean that directory integration should be considered less important just because it's not as difficult. Disparate directories in organizations today are more prevalent than five years ago, so this directory integration functionality has become more logistically complicated, as tools such as TDI have evolved to make the technical aspects simpler. (For a more complete review of the TDI features and functionality, you should refer to the IBM Tivoli Directory Integrator documentation.)

Directory Management Tool (DirLint)

Domino 8 introduces a new tool called DirLint. This tool lets you verify the information that is contained within the directory. It runs against the directory and helps you identify issues, including invalid syntax in names and issues with the naming hierarchy scheme. It also validates that users' names found in groups through Directory Assistance are consistent.

DirLint is a command line utility that is loaded by simply typing, "load dirlint" on the server console. It provides an XML document as output. This document can be read using any Internet web browser.

The information that is produced will be stored in \\Domino\data\IBM\IBM_TECHNICAL_ SUPPORT\lintout_(ServerName)_(Date) as shown above. An example of the information provided in the XML file is as follows:

Authentication through Directory Assistance

In previous releases of Domino, Directory Assistance provided all directories for both authentication and name resolution when addressing messages. This created a situation where ambiguous names would be displayed while a message was being addressed if there was an "authentication only" directory included in the Directory Assistance task. In Domino 8, you have the option through Directory Assistance to specify that the server only references directories contained within the document during the authentication process. This allows you to effectively deploy Directory Assistance for authentication without affecting end users during the addressing of messages.

Basics	Naming Contexts (Rules)	Replicas	
Basics			
Domain type:	Notes		
Domain name:	Comp		
Company name:	Competitive		
Search order:			
Make this domain available to:	☑ Notes Clients & Internet Authentication/ Authorization ☑ LDAP Clients		
Group Authorization:	Yes		
Use exclusively for Group Authorization or Credential Authentication:	Yes		
Enabled:	Yes		

Directory Assistance LDAP Configuration Wizards

Domino 8 offers configuration wizards for LDAP directories. In previous releases, you needed to know a significant amount of information about the LDAP directories that were being connected via Directory Assistance. You still need to understand basic Directory Assistance and LDAP concepts, but the new **Suggest** and **Verify** buttons on the configuration document help you complete the document thus ensuring the proper connectivity to the LDAP servers. Some of the wizard buttons run scripts on the Domino server or connect to the LDAP server directly.

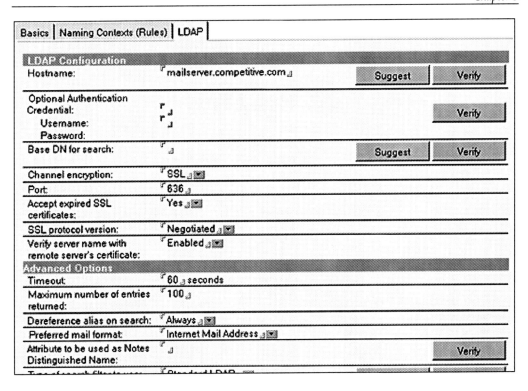

People View by Lotus Notes Version

As users log into Domino, the AdminP process captures the Notes version used to access the server. The information is stored within the Person documents in the Domino Directory.

Notes client machine:	Notes client build:	Notes client platform:	Updated at:
KIDS	Build V70_M4_01112005 Beta	Windows/XP 5.1 Intel Pentium	03/23/2005 07:03:14 PM
37XZUO9CFG	Release 6.5.3	Windows/XP 5.1 Intel Pentium	10/01/2004 09:36:53 AM
HOME	Release 7.0.2	Windows/2000 5.0 Intel	03/26/2007 12:26:11 PM
ISSLKIDS	Release 7.0	Windows/XP 5.1 Intel Pentium	09/06/2005 09:37:24 AM
ISSL	Build V80_M4_03042007NP	Windows/XP 5.1 Intel Pentium	03/22/2007 12:59:12 PM
SERVER	Build V80_M5_05202007	Windows/XP 5.1 Intel Pentium	05/28/2007 10:24:52 PM

The new **People | by Client Version** view allows you to go to the Domino directory and identify the clients that the users are using to access the server. In previous releases, this was a custom view that was needed to be developed and maintained.

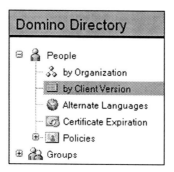

Internet Password Lockout

Domino 8 now offers an Internet password lockout feature. This feature provides a mechanism (via the inetlockout.nsf database) to track all access attempts to the HTTP environment so that the status of the login attempt is logged. The creation of the Internet lockout database can be done manually, during server startup after the process has been configured, upon the first request to view a document, or when a document needs to be created within the database. The only caveat is that the service must have been running for a period of 10 minutes if the server is not to be rebooted.

The Internet password lockout feature can be enabled for the entire environment through a configuration document, or via a policy that more granularly assigns the ability to lockout users from the HTTP access. The configuration setting does the following:

- Enables the feature
- Sets the logging feature to report lockouts, failures, or both
- Sets the maximum number of tries allowed, the lockout expiration timing in minutes, hours and days, and the maximum interval between tries in minutes, hours and days.

The lockout feature only applies to HTTP access, and traditional anti-spoofing mechanism is leveraged within the rich Notes client so that services such as LDAP, POP, IMAP, DIIOP, Lotus Quickplace, and Lotus Sametime are currently not supported with this feature. If your Domino environment is using a customized DSAPI filter, there is a possibility that the Internet password lockout feature will not function, because customized DSAPI filters can be coded to bypass the standard Domino login facility.

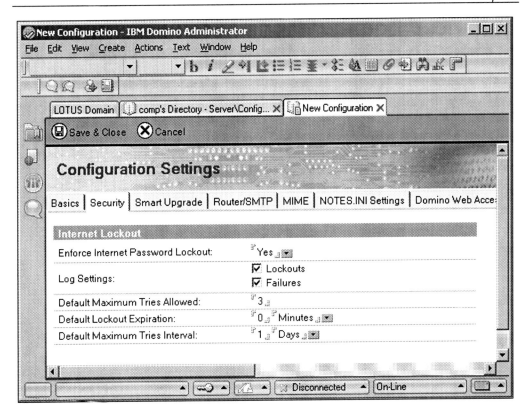

When configuring Internet password lockout via a security policy, the same options are presented as with the configuration document.

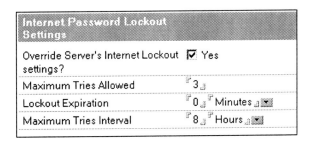

It is important to note that enabling this feature could increase the initial call volume to your Help desk or the administrative overhead required to manage passwords if the HTTP password feature is used significantly within the organization. Also, malicious attacks can occur on the Domino servers through denial of service attacks. This type of an attack could significantly reduce effectiveness within the environment.

Enhanced Local Database Encryption

In Domino 8 the encryption level for all new databases will be set for strong encryption. The ability to encrypt databases with an end user's ID to prevent access by other users' IDs is necessary so as to ensure the protection of data once a database is brought to the local workstation. In previous releases, databases had the ability to be encrypted at the simple, medium, or strong levels, depending on the needs and requirements of the environment and the end users. Domino will still provide backwards compatibility for the simple and medium encryption models, but going forward, all new replicas will be encrypted as strong.

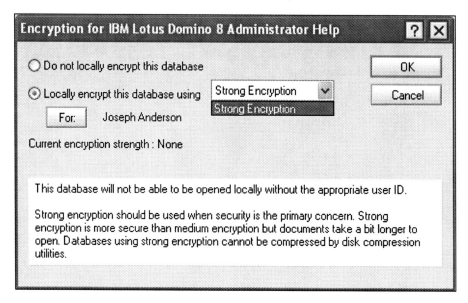

Certifier Key Rollover

Domino administrators can assign a new set of public and private keys to a Domino certificate authority. These keys are used to certify the keys of OUs, servers, and users in that organization. The process of assigning news keys is known as key rollover. Rolling over a CA key may become necessary if the current key is considered too short for adequate encryption, the current key is too old, or if the value of the current private key has been compromised.

When an administrator assigns a new set of keys to a Domino certificate authority, they are created and self-certified and added to the top-level certifier ID file in the pending key area of the ID file. The keys that were previously used are added to the archived keys area of the ID file, and rollover certificates binding the new and old keys are added to the rollover certificate area of the ID file.

In order to support certifier key rollover, the Domino trust model has been extended to include a new type of certificate, rollover certificates. These certificates are issued by an entity to itself. In a hierarchical certificate, there is a single issuer name, a single subject name, and a single subject key. In a rollover certificate, there is a single name (which is both the issuer and the subject) and two subject keys; one key is used to sign the certificate and attests to the fact that the subject name is legitimately in possession of the other key.

Generally, when a key is rolled over, two roll-over certificates are issued; one of them is signed by the old key saying that the new key is valid, and the other is signed by the new key saying that the old key is valid. Each certificate has its own expiration date.

Rollover certificates are essential for limiting the expiration dates of certificates issued to the older keys. One of the reasons for rolling over a key is that a former key has been compromised or considered to be old enough for the danger of compromise to be unacceptable. In such cases, limiting the expiration date of a rollover certificate limits the lifetime of a formerly issued child certificate. This is done by specifying an early enough expiration date in the rollover certificate.

SSO for LTPAToken2

Multi-server session-based authentication, also known as single sign-on (SSO), allows web users to log in once to a Domino or WebSphere server, and then access any other Domino or WebSphere servers in the same DNS domain that are enabled for SSO without having to log in again. The SSO feature makes logging in and using multiple servers in a mixed environment easier for users. Web browsers must have cookies enabled since the authentication token that is generated by the server is sent to the browser in a cookie.

SSO may be set up by creating a domain-wide configuration document in the directory and enabling the multi-servers option for session-based authentication in a web site or a server document.

Certificate Revocation Checking through the Online Certificate Status Protocol (OCSP)

The Online Certificate Status Protocol (OCSP) enables applications to determine the revocation state of an identified certificate. OCSP checks are made during S/MIME signature verification and mail encryption by the Notes client. OCSP is enabled through a policy, using the **Enable OCSP checking** setting on the **Keys and Certificates** tab.

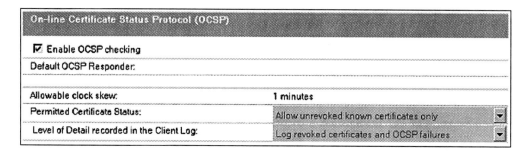

Other new Domino 8 directory/security features include LDAP server improvements for WebSphere Member Manager (WMM) and larger key support.

Enhanced Integration with IBM Servers and Tools

The Notes and Domino environment has continually leveraged other IBM technologies to improve performance, reliability, administration, and functionality. The Domino 8 release has built upon prior successes and added more robust support for other IBM technologies. This section will focus on the integration of DB2, WebSphere Portal, and the Tivoli Enterprise Console.

IBM DB2 as a Back-End Data Store

Lotus Domino 7 introduced the ability to use IBM DB2 software as an alternative to the Lotus Notes storage facility (NSF) for storing Lotus Domino data on a per-database basis. This feature, called the Lotus Domino and DB2 feature, enables you to use both DB2 and Lotus Domino databases, accessing and viewing data stored in either format.

When you run Domino with DB2, there are three distinct interactions that occur between Domino and DB2:

- Domino uses DB2 as an alternate data store for Notes data.
- Specific sets of data are pushed from an NSF to DB2 in the form of DB2 Access Views (DAVs).
- A Notes view can be built based on an SQL query in the form of query views.

Domino 8 introduces two new features for integration with DB2:

- Set or delete default DB2 user name. Domino verifies the uniqueness of the default DB2 user name.
- DB2 Move Container. This allows you to move a DB2 from one disk or volume to another disk or volume so as to control space usage.

IBM WebSphere Portal Integration Wizard

A future release of WebSphere Portal will introduce an enhanced integration wizard that reduces the complexity required to enable Lotus Domino 8 and WebSphere Portal integration. This includes the setting up of the Common PIM (personal information management) portlets (CPP) and the Lotus Domino Extended Products portlets (DEPP).

The wizard will automate the following

- Configure single sign-on (export LTPA token, create Web SSO document on Lotus Domino).
- Configure Lotus Sametime (single sign-on, enable awareness for Lotus Domino Web Access, set up trusted servers in STCENTER.NSF).
- Configure Lotus Domino Directory (single sign-on, DIIOP, configure collaborative services to bind to Lotus Domino LDAP).
- Configure Lotus Domino mail servers (single sign-on, DIIOP, Notes.ini settings for HTTP, enable XML services).

Perhaps the most dramatic improvement is the Notes 8 rich client. Notes and Domino 8 software makes it easy for you to integrate line-of-business solutions and data into a new class of applications, called composite applications. Both Domino 8 and WebSphere Portal 6 servers can host composite applications. This will allow clients to run both Domino applications and portlets (as well as servlets and Internet applications). The following diagram depicts the Notes/Domino infrastructure, a rich client, as well as a web client and necessary components to facilitate this architecture.

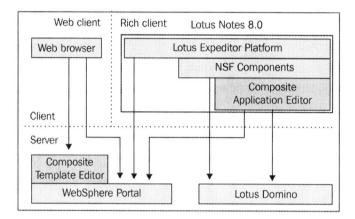

IBM Tivoli Enterprise Console Integration

The Tivoli Enterprise console consolidates events from networks, hardware, and software throughout the environment, and presents them in a single monitoring interface. Domino 7 allowed you to configure events generated by operating system probes to be viewed with other events in the Enterprise console.

Domino 8 allows you to configure any events to be forwarded to the Enterprise console. The first thing you need to do is configure the connectivity to the Tivoli Enterprise Console through the Lotus Domino server configuration document.

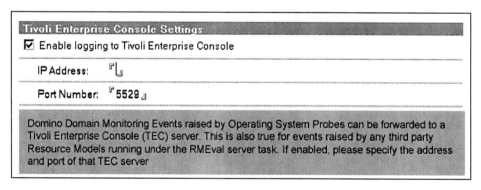

It is then necessary to forward the events to the Tivoli Enterprise Console. You do this by configuring the `events.nsf` database so as to describe the proper Event Handler documents required by the Enterprise console.

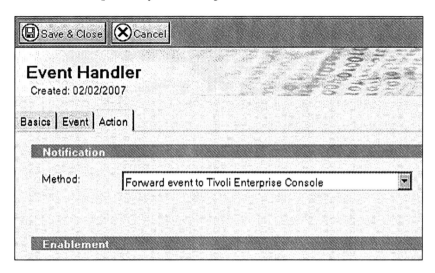

Summary

In this chapter, we took a brief look at the major new and enhanced feature areas in Domino 8. This includes end user and messaging enhancements, administrator enhancements, performance enhancements, directory and security enhancements, and better integration with other IBM technologies.

6

Deployment Enhancements in Notes/Domino 8

The deployment and management of Notes/Domino has traditionally been divided between the Domino administration staff and the desktop management team. In previous releases, the deployment of Notes was a completely stand-alone process, and Domino administrators relied on the desktop team to deploy the client. Domino then introduced a feature called Smart Upgrade to assist with the management and deployment of new Notes client releases. This concept of server-based management of the client was significantly enhanced with the introduction of policies and enhancements to Smart Upgrade.

The task of managing the Notes client through Domino has been significantly enhanced in Notes/Domino 8. With the introduction of the Eclipse client platform for Notes, the Domino server becomes a provisioning tool. Advancements in policies and the introduction of the database redirect feature also significantly improve the ability to manage the Notes environment.

This chapter focuses on the new and improved technologies that allow Domino to better deploy and manage upgrades to the Notes client:

- **Client provisioning** includes new features that leverage Eclipse client and server provisioning.
- **Policy enhancements** include new and enhanced features within the policy document environment.
- **Database redirect** is a new feature that allows you to better manage database access from the end user environment.

Client Provisioning

The shifting of Notes to the Eclipse platform has a significant impact on the end user community. As noted in chapter 2 of this book, the new look and feel of the client and the underlying Eclipse foundation enhances the end user environment. Eclipse-based plug-ins in Notes extend the user's ability to work in a collaborative environment. Unfortunately, the management of these new features may require a higher level of user interaction. Lotus/IBM has recognized this issue, and has leveraged the native Eclipse provisioning architecture to allow for the management of plug-ins and the desktop environment. The introduction of these provisioning features does not replace the Smart Upgrade feature; this utility can still be used to deploy versions of the client.

Server-Managed Provisioning

Domino 8 offers functionality that allows for the deployment of the full Notes client, Eclipse-based plug-ins, and applications (native Domino, composite, or Expeditor based). The following illustration shows the different models for managing the end user environment:

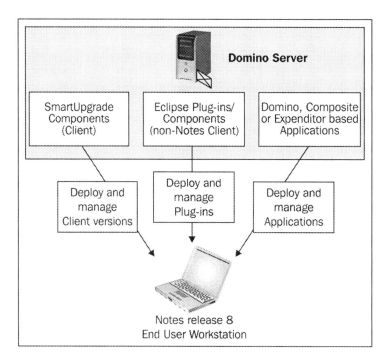

Smart Upgrade

The traditional Smart Upgrade feature within the Domino server can be used to deploy Notes to the end users. The Smart Upgrade feature will assist in pushing the entire set of client code to the Notes user community.

For more information on the Smart Upgrade feature, refer to the Domino 8 Administrator Help database.

Eclipse-Based Provisioning

Notes 8 is built on the Eclipse foundation. Composite applications are considered as features within the Notes architecture, so their deployment and management is handled through the same process as other Eclipse-based features. The management of
Eclipse-based clients such as Notes and Sametime Connect 7.5.x is now shifted to the native provisioning model. When the end user or administrator wants to push out a new feature to Notes, they will be directed to a Site.XML, which contains the information for installing the feature. The feature that is being installed within the Eclipse framework will have dependant plug-ins required for the feature to function properly.

Within Domino 8, a new `update.ntf` template leverages the native Notes replication and security features, to provide and manage access to new and updated features.

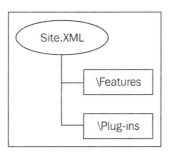

For more information on provisioning features through Domino, consult the Domino 8 Administrator Help database.

Policies

Policies were introduced in earlier releases of Domino to assist in the management of end users through a server-managed process. They are configured through the Domino Directory. Domino 8 introduces new policy documents, as well as new options within existing policy documents. This section will review these new and enhanced policies and options.

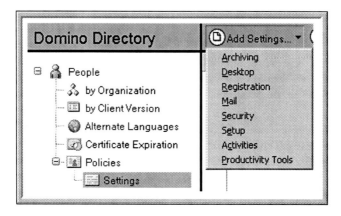

 It is important to note that Domino uses dynamic configuration to deploy all policy settings, with the exception of the mail policy settings. When end users authenticate with their home servers, the information stored within the policy settings documents is deployed (pushed down) to the end users. The mail policy settings are not deployed through the dynamic configuration process; instead they are deployed throughout the environment via the administration process (AdminP).

"How to apply setting" Feature

In previous releases of Domino, policies were applied to all end users who were configured to receive them. This was limiting, as it forced users to conform to the policies without the option of changing them later if necessary. The new **How to apply setting** option allows you to configure whether the policy is applied, using one of the following three options:

- **No policy, use default value**: This option uses the initial configuration upon installation of the client.

- **Set initial value**: This option sets the value for the end user, but does not prohibit the end user from later changing it to better suit current requirements.

- **Set value and prevent changes**: This option sets the value for the end user and enforces the option so that the end user cannot make a change.

Activities Policy Settings Document

Lotus Connections does not require the use of Notes/Domino, but with the Eclipse platform, the Activities portion of the product can be leveraged as a plug-in to the client environment. To support this new product and the plug-in, Domino 8 contains a new Activities policy document to manage the Activities environment, specifically the ability to configure an Activities server URL and port. Additionally, you can specify whether or not SSL is leveraged to encrypt the username, password, and data.

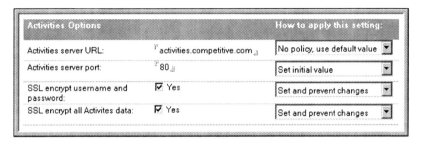

Productivity Tools Settings Document

The support of Open Document Format (ODF) has been extended to Notes/Domino through the introduction of productivity tools within the client. To support this new feature, Domino 8 contains a new productivities tools policy document. This can be used to leverage the tools and macros, and the ability to choose which Microsoft Office and SmartSuite files and templates to open by default.

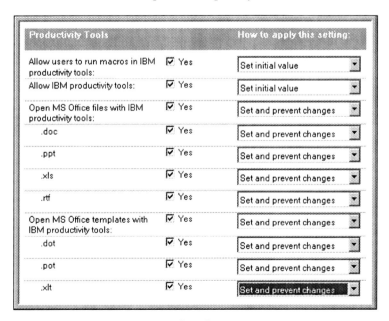

Desktop Policy Settings Document (and Setup Policy Settings Document)

To ease the management of the environment, the options for the setup policy settings document are now also available in the desktop policy settings document. You can now use just one document (the desktop policy settings document) to establish the desktop policy settings as well as many of the setup policy settings. It is recommended that going forward, you use the new, updated desktop policy settings document to define both your desktop policy settings and your setup policy settings.

The desktop policy settings document controls the user's workspace. Desktop settings are enforced the first time a user logs in to Notes and runs setup. After the initial setup, you can use the policy settings to update the user's desktop settings. Users receive updates to the settings when any of the policy settings change; the desktop policy settings are enforced the next time users authenticate with their home server.

Replication Settings through the Desktop and Setup Policy Documents

As customers consolidate their Domino environments, the use of the local replication model is becoming more popular. Local replication allows end users to interact with their mail databases locally on their machines and to leverage the native asynchronous notification process to deliver mail to the workstation.

Deploying the local replication model is the key to the success of the consolidation project. With local replica-based mail, users perform all their mail functions in a replica stored on the hard drive of the workstation. They can use replication to create a local instance of a Domino database on the workstation. Updates such as receiving new mail or template changes are initially received by the server mail replica. The Notes client then pulls these updates to the local database via replication. Any changes that have been made on the local mail replica, such as composing new mail, deleting mail, or putting it in a folder, are pushed to the Domino server after receiving new updates via replication.

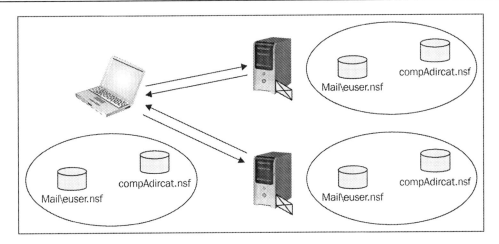

Implementing local replica-based mail allows users to access databases on the workstation without requiring a connection to a Domino server. This approach provides advantages for users who are connected over a wide area network or a virtual private network, since the operations of sending and receiving mail happen without the user noticing. By performing these operations in the background, slight errors in network communication will not be known to the user. Since new messages are kept locally until sent, there will not be any hang conditions in the Notes client when a server connection is slowed or lost.

For the consolidated environment, Notes clients will be configured to connect to a primary and secondary email server at the closest geographic site. The local replication model will be used and new messages will be synchronized with the servers in a high priority replication interval of 5-10 minutes. Addressing services will be provided by a condensed directory replicated to the local Notes client on a normal replication cycle of 30-60 minutes. Applications will be replicated following the normal replication cycle. Notes 8 clients will use the integrated instant messaging services linked to a clustered Sametime instant messaging server.

The desktop policies include a section that allows you to set and enforce replication on end users' workstations. In previous versions of Notes/Domino, there was no way to set and/or enforce replication to the end users desktop. This allowed some users to disable replication or set the replication threshold at one minute or less.

The following diagram outlines the replication settings available through the desktop policy. All options have the new **How to apply this setting** feature to enhance the setting of standards throughout the environment.

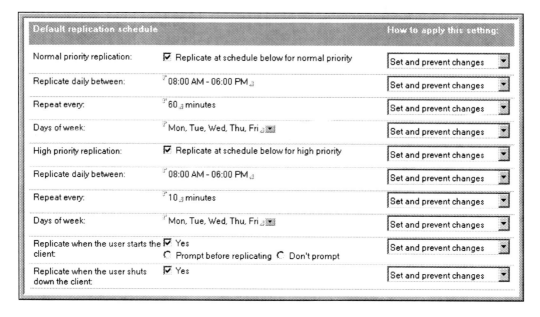

Security Policy Settings Document

The security policy settings document has been enhanced to allow administrators to better manage Notes and Internet passwords, configure password polices, set up key rollover, and manage administration execution control lists (ECLs). In addition to these features, the security policy document in Domino 8 has been enhanced to account for the installation of Eclipse-based plug-ins. There are three options that can be configured within the security policy document within the **Signed Plug-in** tab, as noted below. Each option has the ability to be configured with the options as noted: **Ask the user, Never install,** and **Always install.**

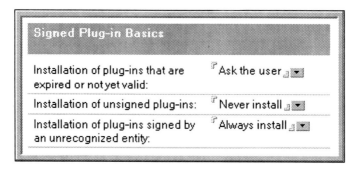

There are a number of other new and enhanced features within the policies environment. Refer to the Domino 8 Administrator Help for more information about this and other topics.

Database Redirect

In previous releases of Notes/Domino, when the administrator moved or deleted a database, it was sometimes difficult to have end users redirect their links to the new location or (in the case of deletion) shift them to a replica. To address this, Domino 8 introduces a new feature called **database redirect**.

Redirect When Databases Are Moved

To redirect a database that is being moved, open the administration client and select the database in the Files tab. Then in the right pane select **Database | Move**.

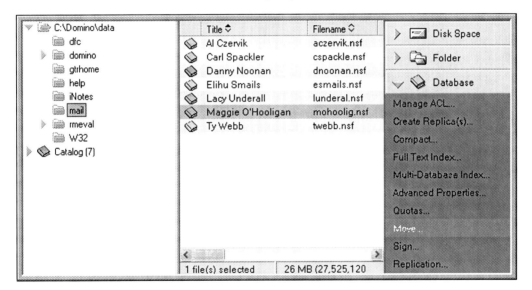

Select the servers to which you want to move the database, and select the directory in which the databases should be placed. In the right-hand pane, select the server, and in the lower right-hand section select **Create a redirect marker for updating client references**. This creates the redirection after the administrative process completes the move.

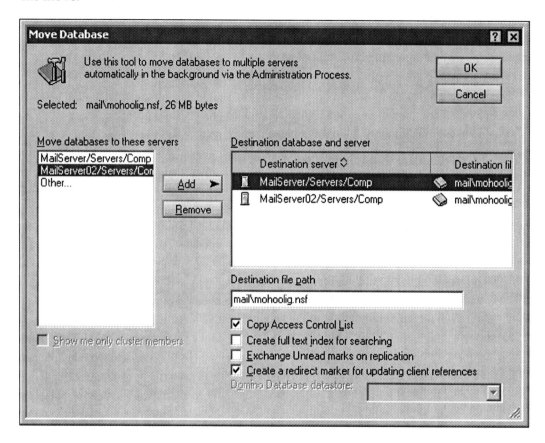

Redirection When Databases Are Deleted

In the administration client **Files** tab, select the database to be moved. Then, in the right pane, select **Database | Delete**.

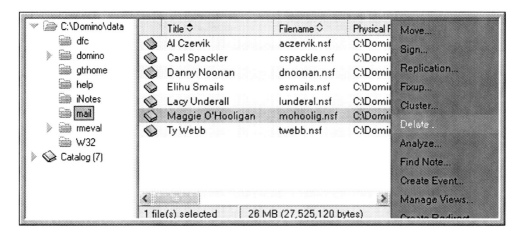

In the dialog box, select the **Create a marker that allows clients to update their references to this database** option.

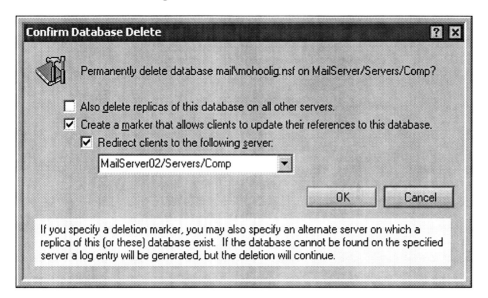

Then choose the server to which users will be redirected to access the database. This is very useful when deleting a database on a specific server where the end user population is known.

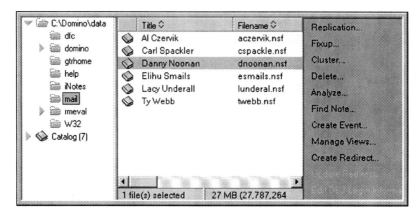

You can then move users to a replica on another server so as to help balance the load within the environment. When the following dialog box is presented, click **Add** to select the replica to which users are to be redirected.

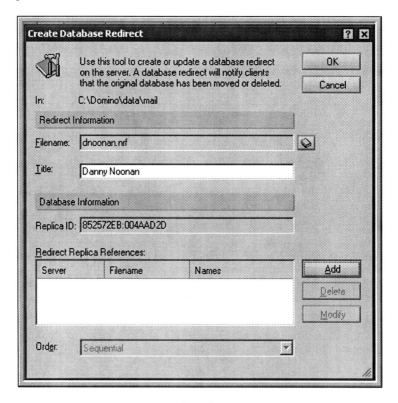

When selecting the database for redirection, you have the option of selecting which users should be redirected to the replica of the database. (This is an optional step in the redirect process.)

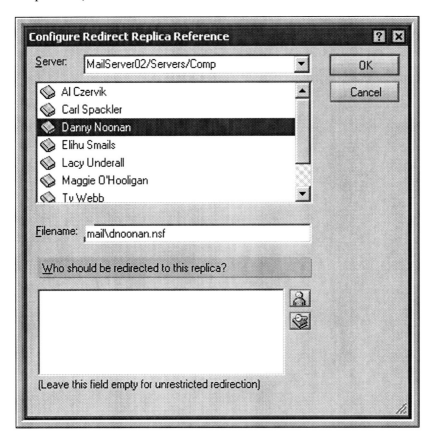

Then select **OK** in the dialog box to confirm the redirect.

Summary

In this chapter, we have examined a number of important Notes/Domino 8 features that can make rolling out your new deployment significantly easier. We discussed client provisioning, including Eclipse-based client and server provisioning functionality. We also looked at policy enhancements and the new database redirect feature.

7

Upgrading to Notes/Domino 8

After you have decided to upgrade to Domino 8, you will need to create an upgrade plan. Most companies are not able to upgrade all users and servers at once. There are several things that you need to consider before you upgrade. This chapter explains these things. Overall, the upgrade process from Notes 6 or Notes 7 client is relatively easy. You can use the SmartUpgrade process to help upgrade these clients. (See chapter 6 for more details on SmartUpgrade.)

This chapter is divided into two main sections. In the first, we look at the Notes/Domino upgrade process in general, discussing concepts and steps that should be considered whenever you upgrade to any major release of Notes/Domino. In the concluding section, we look at upgrade issues that are specific to Notes/Domino 8.

The Domino/Notes Upgrade Process

The Domino/Notes upgrade process consists of a number of phases, as follows:

- Vision and direction.
- High-level architecture analysis
- Use cases.
- Requirements.
- Agreements.
- Final target architecture.
- Creating the design and upgrade plans.
- Creating test plan.
- Testing.
- Creating upgrade process document and plans.

- Executing logistics plans and schedules.
- Creating the pilots.
- Updating and final changes.

We discuss each of these phases below.

Vision and direction: This phase is where you define your goals for the upgrade. These goals can include your business needs, a basic idea of your current IT architecture, and some rough time lines for the upgrade. A simple vision charter might read something like this:

> *THE COMPANY will upgrade their ND5/6/7 architecture to Domino 8 in X months, taking advantage of new Domino 8 features, and will also consolidate several servers during the upgrade.*

High-level architecture analysis: Before you upgrade, make sure you know what you have. Experience tells us that most companies cannot identify 100% of their environment. A good review is prudent so as to keep surprises to a minimum. Take the time to obtain a list of applications, including email applications and custom applications, backup systems, virus scanners, and web-based services and appliances. Build an inventory of all things that "touch" Domino. This will help you identify any items that may be affected impacted by the upgrade.

Use cases: A use case, in this context, is a statement and description of a system/ service that defines the use and behavior of an environment. A basic use case should include the following elements:

- Upgrade steps
- Description of requirements
- Goals to help target requirements
- Identification of "actors" (the people using the system: users, administrators, operators, and so on)
- Identification of associations between use cases and actors

These documents will help you build a set of requirements. In each use case, you should also identify various states of the upgrade. Examples include upgrading the servers, and enabling the new mail policy feature once all of the clients and server have been upgraded.

A use case can point to the need for:

- Client upgrade
- Server upgrade
- ODS upgrade (optional with Domino 8)
- Communications and transformation management
- Application upgrade
- Custom API upgrades
- Calendaring and Scheduling (including rooms and resources)
- Administration tool upgrade
- SMTP service upgrade
- Security impacts
- Directory impacts
- Process upgrade
- Help desk

A sample use case is included at the end of this chapter.

Requirements: When all the use cases have been created and agreed on, you can summarize them into a total list of requirements. These use cases and requirements can be used to determine upgrade steps, use of new features, systemic impacts, budgets, and time-lines. These requirements will be used to create the "draft" target architecture.

Agreements: This is where you will build out your budgets, build out decision records, and obtain agreements from all interested parties in your organization. After all of the agreements have been approved and signed, then your target architecture can be finalized.

Final target architecture: At this point, the final target architecture can be created. In most organizations, there will normally be a phased approach. It can take several iterations to get to this final architecture. One example would be new Domino 8 programming functions. In order to take advantage of this feature, you will need to have both servers and clients upgraded before the new functions are enabled.

Create the design and upgrade plans: This step is where you start the process to detail the upgrade process. Also, you begin documenting the process that will be used as a step-by-step upgrade guide.

Create test plan: Remember the identification of new features and requirements? This is where you create a test plan to test each of the upgrade elements, which includes the server, clients, applications, custom tools, and other items

Testing: The flowchart below shows the testing and pilot process:

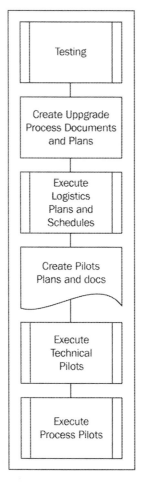

Each part of the upgrade should be tested before you actually put any new technology into a production environment. Most companies execute what are known as "unit" or component tests. These tests are the basic components of the new technology. For example, you might choose to test the Notes 8 client on a sampling of your current PCs. This particular test verifies that Notes 8 will run on your exiting hardware, and does not impact any other applications and/or PC environment. As testing progresses, you will start to include each other element into the environment, for example, Notes 8 on the network, Notes 8 on applications, Notes 8 client that will access a Domino 6 or 7 server, and so on.

The goal is to test Notes/Domino in a holistic test environment that replicates various part of your production environment.

 One very important step is to contact each vendor for any third-party tools and utilities. The upgrade process will make changes to the directory, and then to each server. Be sure to contact every vendor and determine whether or not Domino 8 (or any new release of Notes/ Domino) is support by that vendor. Double-check to verify that APIs have been recompiled (as needed) by the vendor, and that the new directory is supported. Then do your own testing, to make sure all is working as advertised by the vendor.

Create upgrade process document and plans: Create all of the upgrade steps, procedures, and schedules, training, and Frequently Ask Questions documents. Some of these documents will be the actual upgrade steps and checklists. If you are upgrading a large number of servers and users, then you can use a tracking database and/or spreadsheet. The results of the testing will be manifest in the upgrade process. Also, communications plans should be created at this time.

Execute logistics plans and schedules: This is where you order any equipment, hire any additional staff, and start the overall upgrade process. Included in the scheduling process will be the execution of the pilots. (See the following step.)

Create the pilots: Next, create and document each pilot that is needed. You will need two pilot types: non-production pilots (technical pilots, process pilots), and production pilots (shown in the diagram later in this chapter).

As we mentioned earlier, you should test as much as possible in a test environment before executing a production roll-out. These non-production pilots are an opportunity to test each step of a process. These should include:

- Upgrade steps.
- Training and education.
- Communications.
- Help desk testing and FAQ.
- Executive help staff.

One important step of the pilots is "lessons learned". Each pilot is an opportunity to modify upgrade steps and processes.

Non-production pilots are normally separated into two types, technical pilots and process pilots. Technical pilots verify that each holistic step of the upgrade works correctly. Process pilots verify that the actual checklists and documents are correct.

Transformation management: When upgrade/migration projects fail, it is always people issues, not technical problems, which are the root cause. Transformation management (TM) is a formal process to help identify and mitigate the people issues associated with each project. Change is implied by any upgrade and/or migration. TM takes into considerations the various work environment issues that occur during the upgrade/migration project. One core fundamental part of any TM plan is communication.

Here is a simple example that could form the basis of the communication part of a TM plan:

Your company is taking on a migration/upgrade to Domino 8. Your company may experience a few changes to the architecture, some changes to end user clients, and possibility a few changes to the administration teams. In some cases the end user and administrators may require some training on Notes and Domino 8. Your company should consider the following activities as part of the administration and migrations team's transformation management activities:

1. Develop a team name: for example, *The Domino8 Upgrade Team*. (Also create a team logo.)

2. Develop a team charter: for example, Migrate/upgrade x number of users in n number of weeks.

3. Announce the date of the final "migration done" party.

4. Create an intranet web site with a list of FAQs, and the names and pictures of the migration team members.

5. Create a Red/Yellow team to isolate the migration team from the end users (post-migration issues).

6. Develop two sets of communications from the migration team to end users. This should be added to the overall TM planning.

7. Introduce users to the migration team. These users will be notified about the migration team and their purpose. Also users should be instructed about whom they should contact with questions about the upcoming migration. LPS/ISSL recommends that the help desk be trained about the migration and possible end user questions.

8. A pre-migration FAQ should be created and hosted on the Intranet.

9. Print posters with the name of the team and the logo on the top of the poster, and place them where they are likely to be seen (break rooms, elevators, and so on).

---

10. After users have been migrated, send out a weekly message to migrated users, with "Tips of the week" and other relevant information.

11. Three milestone meetings will be needed for your company's migration/upgrade:

    ○ The opening meeting: The CIO or CEO should open this meeting. A quick five-minute pep talk is all that is needed from the VPs, but it could be important for the team to let them know that there is executive support. The lead project manger will launch the migration. Announce the plans, hand out procedures, and review the whole process.

    ○ The "half-way" meeting: This occurs when 50% of users migrated have been migrated. This is a great cause of celebration, so give out some special awards!

    ○ The final party: At the "98% of users migrated" mark, close out the migration. Move the remainder of the migration processes into the permanent support staff.

12. Close out the project.

13. Transfer any left over migrated users into the current customer steady state support staff.

A "go/no go" decision is made before the production pilots are executed. This decision will be based on the results of the testing and pilots. If all have been successful, then the next step will be the production pilots.

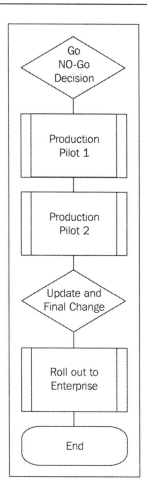

Once all of the pilots had been completed, you will need to start the actual upgrade process. Use a set of "friendly" users (never use executives!) for the first pilot. The preceding diagram shows two production pilots. In reality, you will execute as many as are needed. Each pilot will provide lessons learned to be used for the next pilot.

Update and final changes: After all the pilots have been executed, and you have had an opportunity to update the processes and make any final changes to the overall upgrade process, you will be ready to roll out the upgrade to your enterprise.

Notes/Domino 8 Upgrade

So far we have discussed a generic Domino/Notes upgrade process. In this section, we discuss the specific upgrade issues for Notes/Domino 8.

Reviewing the Current Infrastructure (the Health Check)

Before you upgrade you will need to identify the components and systems that will be impacted by this upgrade. This is an opportunity for you to execute a system wide heatlh check – this normally includes a review of the following:

- **Servers**: Identify any existing issues, such as crashes, problem servers, and slow access. Your servers should be tested before you process the upgrade. Be sure to set up similar servers in a test environment, and use server.load to test the performance capabilities of your servers. Also, make sure that your servers are not "sick"; you should not upgrade a server that is crashing or having hardware issues. Fix issues and problems before you upgrade.

- **Monitoring systems** (Tivoli, DDM, BMC, and so on): There are many new monitoring features with Domino 8. Be sure that your current monitoring systems work with Domino 8, and that there are no conflicts with any new features.

- **Directory architecture** (directory analysis, directory customization): This is a big step. Analyze you directory, and determine whether or not there is any customization. Determine whether or not any custom design features (views, forms, and so on) need to be moved into a new directory. In some cases, you may find these customizations are no longer needed in Domino 8.

- **Clients**: Test you clients, and make sure that your current hardware and software configuring will support Notes 8.

- **PDA and/or other wireless systems**: with each new release, new features are added. Be sure to verify that any new features don't conflict with your PDA devices. For example, we have seen in the past where a ODS change broke the connection between the local PDA and the data on the Notes Client.

- **AdminP status**: This is a great opportunity to makes sure that `admin4.nsf` is replicating to all servers, and that all AdminP ACL database assignments are correct. Also, there are new features that allow you to set up several directory AdminP servers using Extended Directory access control.

- **Application analysis**: This includes any issues with applications being upgraded, custom templates, and API analysis. Be sure to test your applications with Domino 8. In general, upgrading to Domino 8 should not result in any issues relating to existing applications, but it's always a good idea to test with any upgrade. Make sure that your custom APIs still work as needed with Domino 8. In some cases, you may need to recompile some of these APIs, and in other cases, you may no longer need the APIs.

- **Custom templates**: Check for customization of system templates. Compare this customization with any new features in Domino 8, and determine whether or not you need to move this customization into the templates and applications. The use of the IVES Team Studio Delta tool will help you with your analysis.

- **Messaging architecture** (including NRPC services, SMTP services, messaging tracking, enterprise-wide communications, mass mail, corporate communication, and co-existence with other messaging systems and other tools): NRPC rarely causes problems during or after upgrades, but it's never a bad idea to test this anyway. Make sure that NRPC Notes Name Networks (a.k.a. NNN) or Domino Named Networks (DNN) work as before the upgrade. Test each SMTP Services feature that is enabled. Test each Domino message tracking feature that is enabled in your current environment. There are a wide variety of mass-mailing tools and other customized features that may be installed in your environment. Be sure to test each of these tools. Large enterprise organizations can have several varieties of mail systems and servers. Test any custom interfaces, software, and SMTP connectivity. Be sure and check out the new "out of office" configuration features for ND8 – you now have the option of using the router to launch the "out of office" messages in place of the standard agent.

- **Other services and servers**: There are a large number of Lotus/IBM products. All of these need to be tested. Examples include Quickplace, Sametime, LEI, SMTP gateways, virus scanners, backup services, and provisioning systems. Ensure that these products (and the versions you have installed) are supported with Domino/Notes 8:

- **Domino replication** (activity logging, replication topology, replication settings, connection documents, access control, replication schedules, cluster replication, if enabled): Our experience with most upgrades is there is rarely an issue with replication and upgrades, but be sure to test this.

- **Messaging topology** (server topology, named networks, domains, inbound and outbound message flow, routing requirements, routing priorities, volume metrics, client strategy, server vs. local replication, alternate client access [POP, IMAP, web, mobile users], hand-held device recommended practices [Treo vs. Blackberry]): With ND7 a new task was added: the Room and Resource manager task; be sure and test your Rooms and Resources architecture as part of your upgrade.

- **Mail-enabled applications**: Most Domino architectures will have several mail-enabled applications. These can, and will, be affected by an upgrade to a new release of Domino. Overall, Lotus Notes and Domino provides great backward compatibility, but you still need to exercise due diligence regarding any new Lotus Script elements, new "@Functions", and new design elements. At the minimum, verify that the mail-in-DB records are functioning correctly.

- **Architecture** (high level review, connections to internal systems [networks, unified messaging, SMTP/Internet domains]).

- **Network** (platforms, DNS/DHCP, remote access): Overall, we see very little impact to this area with an upgrade. Again, take the time to test the new release to make sure that the 'basics' work.

- **Calendar & scheduling** (user calendaring [delegation, manager access], enterprise scheduling [resources, shared group calendars]).

- **Directory** (directory architecture [in particularly directory design], directory management, directory synchronization, naming [Servers, users, O and OUs]).

- **Security** (ACL access, anonymous access, encryption and certificates, certification practice statement, organization structure, ID management, access controls [file server system, console and physical, server access/pass-thru/deny, client execution control, administration access]).

- **Capacity**: Determine if servers can handle current user loads (mail file size, hardware sizing), load balancing/sage, and capacity planning. Our experience is that each new release of Domino provides better performance in CPU and memory, and that each new release provides more features. With each new feature or function you will find additional resources being used – in particular, system memory. Be sure to monitor, via statistical baselines, the impact of a new release on the current setup of hardware.

- **Configuration settings**: These are a very important part of the server upgrade. Review each server configuration to determine if you need to make any changes.

- **Environmental variables**: Check for abandoned Notes.ini variables and obsolete notes.ini settings. Check the on-line support tools for this list. The release notes may also have some information about the current set of supported Notes.ini variables.

- **Management and administration** (change control, administration model, client management, remote access recommendations, staffing levels, service monitoring and reporting, systems management, backup and restore model).

- **ESX/VmWare**: There are a number of Domino enterprises that are looking at ESX and WMware. At the time of writing, there are limited sets of data regarding the successful use of ESX for Domino 'messaging'. If you are considering using ESX for ND8 messaging, we suggest the following:

  - Review the current supportability statements (URL and release notes) from IBM on this topic.

- ○ If possible, do not upgrade to both ND8 and ESX/WMware at the same time. This is the old rule of not making too mange changes at once

- ○ Be sure to set up a test lab to check how ESX will work with a shared CPU and memory model. Also pay close attention to the Disk I/O queues. Server.load can help you with test loads/scripts.

If you are using clustering, you should monitor the workqueue depth and seconds on queue statistics.

The Upgrade Process

After you have checked the infrastructure, it is time to start the upgrade. The following steps show the basic upgrade path. This path can vary, based on your research and the use cases that you have created:

Systemic normalization: The first step of your upgrade is to "normalize" your architecture. We have already mentioned that it is important not to make any changes, upgrades or migrations to an environment that is "sick". Take the time to review each health check category and determine if your environment is stable. If it is stable, you can then upgrade your architecture.

Upgrade the Domino Administrator clients: Upgrade all of your Domino Administrator clients. Verify that all feature and functions run in the current environment before you upgrade your first server.

Upgrade the Domino directory: This step can be executed before you upgrade your first server. Remember the use case above? Use that to drive the upgrade of the directory, making any customizations and changes. Be sure to work with IBM/Lotus support to make sure that the directory is backward-compatible with your current directory. (You should have done this in the testing phase of the upgrade.)

Upgrade the administration server: This is a very important server. AdminP requires that you assign an administration server to the Domino directory (`names.nsf`).

The AdminP server task runs on all Domino servers. This task loads when the Domino server is first started, and is controlled through the `notes. ini` variable ServerTasks. The AdminP server task wakes up on periodic time intervals (specified in the Administration Process section of the Server document) and executes commands waiting in the Administration Request database. Each command placed in the Administration Request database has an assigned proxy action. These proxy actions are essentially the op-code that runs the administration process. Each command placed in the administration request database is represented by a document. Each document has a number of fields, including one called Proxy Action. After each action has completed on a server, a response document is created to indicate the status of that request.

There is a new option (since release 7) to use multiple servers to maintain the Domino directory. If a Domino domain is geographically dispersed, then you can use several servers to process administration requests:

Carefully evaluate your Administration server: Due to the new complexities of Domino 8 and some new proxy actions, you may need to have a dedicated administration server. AdminP can generate a large number of proxy actions as your architecture grows.

Upgrade utility servers: This step can be different with each customer. In some cases, the hub server can be upgraded first, then the utility servers. Utility servers are defined as SMTP, support, tools, and other servers. In some cases, vendors may not be ready with their updates to support a new release of Domino.

Upgrade hub servers: Upgrade each server, and then monitor the "normal" operations between each upgrade. Verify that replication is still working, that agents are still executing, and that mail is still routing.

Upgrade spoke/messaging servers: After the hub servers have been completed, upgrade your spoke and messaging servers.

Upgrade specialized servers: In some cases, these may be some of the first servers you upgrade. One example would be specialized backup software. Once again, you need to contact you vendor before you upgrade your first server or upgrade the directory. The issue is backward compatibility. Verify with each vendor that the tools and utilities will work with each release.

Upgrade the application servers: One important step is to test the applications before you upgrade. There are several tools listed in the reference section of this book that will help you.

Upgrade Notes clients: You are now at the point where you can upgrade the Notes clients. Smart-upgrade can be used if you have Notes/Domino 6/7 installed. If not, you can use a MSI/MST type installs process to roll out the code.

Implement new Domino 8 features: When all servers and clients have been upgraded, you can implement the new Domino 8 features. Each feature should be tested, and in some cases you may need to build an architecture/design for each feature. One new feature that you should consider is the mail policy. This is a new policy that can be enabled after you have upgraded both servers and clients.

Upgrade applications: When your architecture is pure Domino/Notes 8, you can start to implement new Domino 8 features in your applications. Use the testing methodology listed above.

Special Feature Upgrade Considerations

Lotus Notes and Domino 8 include a number of important new features. These features are discussed in Chapters 2 and 3 in this book. Be sure to consider these features as part of your upgrade planning:

Productivity tools: Notes 8 includes a set of office productivity tools which support the Open Document Format (ODF) standard. These include IBM Lotus Documents (create, edit, and share word processing documents), IBM Lotus Presentations (create and deliver presentations), and IBM Lotus Spreadsheets (create spreadsheets and analyze numerical data).

LOB: Notes/Domino 8 also makes it easier to integrate line-of business (LOB) solutions and data into new types of applications, called **composite applications**. Composite applications, which are manifested in the front end of a Service Oriented Architecture (SOA) (See chapter 3.)

Mail recall: This is a "planned" option of Domino 8. Work with your administrator to determine if you can use this feature and what options are available.

Improved "out of office" capabilities: This includes an option to specify special hours in addition to specific dates. Now notifications can be sent almost immediately if a person has enabled the "out of office" agent.

Central management: Domino 8 offers the option to centrally managing initial deployment and upgrades of Notes 8 client software and composite applications. Using server-managed provisioning, you can even deploy different Notes 8 client features to different users. This new capability will support the existing Notes SmartUpgrade feature. (Refer to Chapter 6.)

DB2: Domino 7 introduced an option to use IBM DB2 as an alternative to the traditional Lotus Notes storage facility (NSF) for storing Lotus Domino databases. Domino 8 will now support DB2 as part of a standard install.

Use Case Document Example

The following is an example of a use case document. You can use this example as a guideline when creating your own use case documents, which is an important step in the Domino 8 upgrade process.

Example Use case – Domino Server Upgrade.

Use case

Domino Server Upgrade

Subject area

This use case identifies the basic steps needed to upgrade the messaging servers from Notes/Domino 6.x (or 5.x) to Domino 8.

Business event

The upgrade will provide new TCO and management features to your company.

Actors

- Architecture team
- End user
- ISSL
- Administration team
- Operations

Use case overview

These use case deals with the architecture

Help and support

Be sure to checkout the following sites for help and support from IBM and Lotus.

Upgrade Central:
`http://www-306.ibm.com/software/lotus/support/upgradecentral/index.html`

Forums:
`http://www.ibm.com/developerworks/lotus`

Summary

In this chapter, we presented a high-level overview of the steps involved in upgrading your Notes/Domino environment to release 8. We began with a generic description of the Notes/Domino upgrade process. We then concluded with tasks and considerations specific to upgrading your environment to Notes/Domino 8. We also included an example use case that you can use as a template for your own use cases, as well as links to sites that can provide you with additional Notes/Domino 8 upgrade information.

8

Coexistence between Notes/ Domino Releases

This chapter discusses coexistence between Notes/Domino 8 and earlier versions. When you install a new release, there are several things to consider relating to coexistence with earlier releases of Notes/Domino. For example, always test coexistence scenarios before implementing changes in your production environment. Follow the recommended upgrading routine described in chapter 7. Be sure to check with http://www.ibm.com/developerworks/lotus to find the most recent Tech Notes and articles on coexistence.

The first section of this chapter covers Notes client coexistence issues. The second deals with Domino server considerations.

Notes Client Coexistence

Although running two different releases of the Notes client on one workstation is an unsupported configuration, it can be done. The Notes 8 install program will automatically upgrade any existing Notes client. But you can install Notes 8 on a PC, while retaining the previous version of the Notes client.

In the following section, we assume that Notes 7 is installed in the default Windows Client for e-business locations (C:\Notes for programs, and C:\Notes\Data for the data directory). If you run Notes 7 from another directory (such as C:\Program Files\Lotus\Notes, the default Notes 7 product install location), substitute this directory name in place of references to C:\Notes in the description below.

If you want to save your existing Notes 7 (or 6) client binaries, but still want to share the data directory (which is the easiest to use and switch between), you should do the following.

Copy the existing Notes directory and subdirectories to a Notes 7 directory. You only need to copy the Notes directory and the JVM, license, MUI, and xmlschemas sub-directories, not the data subdirectories, but it is easier to copy all directories and subdirectories if you have the space.

1. Create a new desktop shortcut to run the Notes 7 version. To do this:

2. Create a copy of your existing Notes desktop shortcut icon, then right-click on it and choose **Properties**.

3. Change the **Shortcut** tab **Target** value to:
   `<path>\notes7\notes.exe =<path>\notes\notes.ini`
   (This indicates Notes 7 executables using the Notes 8 Notes.ini file and data.)

4. Change the **Start in** value to be:
   `<path>\notes7`

5. Change the **Title** (General tab) to Notes 7.

6. Click **OK** to close the properties dialog.

7. Install the Notes 8 client.

The Notes 8 install will upgrade the original Notes directory and subdirectories to Notes 8 (leaving your Notes 7 copy alone).

If you want to save your existing Notes 7 client binaries *and* data, keeping two separate data directories and Notes.ini files, then perform the following:

Copy the existing Notes directory and subdirectories to a Notes7 directory. Edit your notes7\notes.ini file, replacing any references to \notes\ with \notes7\.

1. Create a new desktop shortcut to run the Notes 7 version.

2. Create a copy of your existing Notes desktop shortcut icon, then right-click on it and choose **Properties**.

3. Change the **Shortcut** tab **Target** value to:
   `<path>\notes7\notes.exe =<path>\notes7\notes.ini`
   (This indicates Notes 7 executables using the Notes 7 Notes.ini and data.)

4. Change the Start in value to be: `<path>\notes7`.

5. Change the **Title** (General tab) to Notes 7.

6. Click **OK** to close the properties dialog.

Install the Notes 8 client. The Notes 8 install will upgrade the original Notes directory to Notes 8, but you will still have a separate copy of your Notes 7 binaries and data.

Usually, you would upgrade Notes clients, after upgrading your Domino servers. This way, Notes users can take advantage of the new features that exist on the server, such as mail message recall (which also requires that the mail template be a Notes 8 design).

There are actually two new Notes clients: the Notes 8 Eclipse based interface and the Notes 8 basic client. The basic client cannot utilize the Eclipse based technology, such as productivity tools, vertical preview pane, composite applications, the Sidebar, and mail improvements related to recent contacts (such as drop-down addressing). This basic client should be used on low memory workstations that do not meet the higher requirements of the Notes 8 Eclipse client. The following table compares the client requirements.

	Notes 7	**Notes 8 Eclipse**
Memory	128 MB minimum	Windows XP 512 MB minimum
	256 MB or more recommended	1 GB or more recommended
		Windows Vista 1GB minimum
	(Windows 2000 and Windows XP)	1.5 GB or more recommended
		Linux 512 MB minimum
		1 GB or more recommended
Disk space	275 MB required	Windows 900 MB required, more recommended
		Linux 1.5 GB required, more recommended
Processor	Pentium or better	Pentium or better

 For more information on the features that are not available in the Notes 8 basic client, consult the Notes 8 release notes.

The requirements for Notes Eclipse are stricter due to the number of enhancements to the client code.

Calendaring and Scheduling

Many of the new features in Notes 8 require the server, the client, and mail file design to all be at the release 8 code-streams to function properly. As a result, most of this new functionality will be unavailable to users until all three are upgraded.

Calendar Delegation

Calendar delegation occurs when an owner of a calendar gives another user access to their calendar for the purpose of managing it (for example, a manager giving access to an assistant). These users require special planning when upgrading to Notes 8. The best practice is to upgrade the clients of the delegate and owner at the same time. We also recommend upgrading the templates at the same time. This will limit issues that can occur if the clients do not have the same release.

Domino Server Coexistence

This section discusses co-existence between Domino 8 and previous versions of Notes/Domino. This will occur as soon as you upgrade your first server. This state is called a **mixed environment** due to the existence of Domino 8 server code as well as pre-Domino 8 code.

Domino Directory

One of the first things to do is to upgrade the design of the Domino directory to Notes/Domino 8. This can be done in advance of the server code upgrade or at the same time as you upgrade your administration server. The Domino 8 directory design is supported on Domino 6.5.x and 7.x servers. There are Domino 8 features that may not function on pre-Domino 8 servers. These features are mostly found in the server and configuration documents.

If you have applications that rely on custom views in your Domino directory, we recommend that you test your applications with the new Domino directory design. If possible, before upgrading from a previous release, clean up any unneeded views and agents in the existing Domino directory. After the design of the Domino directory has been upgraded, the next phase is to upgrade the server code.

ODS

In Domino 8 the default ODS is the same as in Notes/Domino 6 and 7. There is a new optional ODS in Domino 8, ODS48. This new ODS is optional, and should be applied if you ned to utilize these new features.

Administration Requests and Events Databases

After you upgrade your server the administration requests database (`admin4.nsf`) and events database (`events4.nsf`) will automatically be upgraded. There should be no issues due to having the design of these upgraded databases replicate to the other servers.

Rooms and Resource Reservation Database

The rooms and resource reservations database has not changed from Notes/Domino 7. If you are upgrading from Domino 7, then you will not need to make any changes. If you are upgrading from the Domino 6.x code stream, some changes will be necessary. Resource reservation databases with a design of 6.x or earlier are not supported on the Domino 8 server. In releases prior to Notes/Domino 7, the router was the task that processed reservations in the resource reservation database.

Starting in Notes/Domino 7, there is a new task that performs this duty, the Rooms and Resource Manager task (`RNRmgr`). This new task was added to prevent some of the issues that were seen when the router task was used, such as double booking. For instructions on upgrading from the Domino 6.x code stream, see the *Notes and Domino 7 Upgrade Best Practices Red Paper*.

Domino Domain Monitoring

Domino Domain Monitoring (DDM) was first introduced in Domino 7. Most DDM probes do not function on a pre-Domino 7 server. There are also some new probes that are specific to new features and functions in Domino 8. The probes that are specific to the Domino 8 features will not work on pre-Domino 8 servers. For more information on DDM, see red paper *Lotus Domino Domain Monitoring*. For the new features in DDM in Domino 8, refer to the Domino 8 administrator help.

Policies

There are several new policies that have been introduced in Domino 8. New policies that were introduced in Domino 7 or 8 will not be recognized by Notes 6.5.x or earlier clients. Newer policies will not adversely affect the earlier client; they will not be recognized or enforced until the client is upgraded to Notes 8.

Message Recall

While in a mixed environment, if message recall functionality is enabled, users will not be able to recall a message to a user on a pre-Domino 8 server. Message recall is enabled by default.

Cluster Coexistence

A new feature in Domino 8 is streaming replication. You can read more about this new feature in chapter 5 of this book. In a mixed cluster, this feature will not work. Both servers attempting to replicate in the cluster need to be at the Domino 8 code stream in order for streaming replication to occur. In a mixed cluster, the Domino 8 server will attempt to initiate streaming replication. When it cannot do so, it will fail and revert back to regular replication. Cluster replication will function as it did before the upgrade and mixed cluster state. Once two or more of the servers in the cluster have been upgraded to Domino 8, streaming replication will automatically occur between them.

In Domino 8, there have been some minor changes to the cluster database directory or CLDBDIR.nsf. These changes are all backward compatible with pre-Domino 8 servers. You can have mixed releases in a cluster. However, we suggest you upgrade the cluster mates in quick succession.

There have been changes to the "Out of Office" functionality. Now there is the option of having the "Out of Office" feature as a service rather than as an agent. If one of the servers in the cluster is running pre-Domino 8 code, the "Out of Office" feature must be run as an agent.

Domino Web Access

Domino web access requires two things to work properly. The first is the mail file template. In Notes/Domino 8, the mail template is built into Domino web access. There is no longer a separate mail file template for all Domino web access. The second things that is needed is the Forms database. This database is release-based – new features are added to it with each release. In Notes/Domino 8, the Forms database is called forms8.nsf. So if you upgrade the template to Domino 8, make sure that there is such a file on the server. To be backward compatible, a Domino 8 server will include a forms6.nsf file and a forms7.nsf file. This allows you to keep mail files in an earlier template version and still have Domino web access on the Domino 8 server.

When upgrading from R5, Domino 8 will not remove the `forms5.nsf` file. This will allow Domino web access on release 5 to work. If you need Domino web access on release 5 to work on a new installation of Domino 8, you should either place an operating system level copy of the `forms5.nsf` file on the server or replicate a copy.

ID Files

In each past release, there have been changes to the encryption key length so as to provide enhanced security. Older keys can be used on new clients, but they are not forward compatible. This means that newer keys cannot be used on older clients. It is advisable to upgrade your ID files after you have completed your entire upgrade to Notes/Domino 8. This will provide you with the enhanced security offered by the longer key length.

Summary

In this chapter, we examined a few coexistence issues involved with running Notes/Domino 8 in a mixed environment with one or more previous releases. We began with a look at Notes client coexistence. We explained how to install two different versions of Notes on a workstation, and discussed potential issues with calendaring and scheduling in a multi-release environment. We concluded with a discussion of Domino 8 server coexistence, including features such as the Domino directory, ODS, Domino web access, DDM, and ID files.

9
What's New in Notes/ Domino 8 Development

For the past 20 years Lotus Notes and Domino have been the premier collaborative application platform of choice. Small businesses and Fortune 50 companies alike are using the Notes/Domino application platform for email, calendaring and scheduling, instant messaging and applications.

There are hundreds of IBM business partners supporting the community of approximately 130 million users with their daily blogs, web sites, podcasts, and support forums. Any visit to LotusSphere, the IBM's premier end-user conference for the Lotus brand, will leave your head spinning with a myriad of possibilities to integrate Notes/Domino with other technologies in your business.

So, what exactly is the strategy for the future of Notes/Domino development? Given that IBM has a history of protecting their user's investments in the platform, the strategy is obviously one of extension of the platform while continuing to support legacy applications.

All of the applications written for the platform have one thing in common, the end user. The end user operates in a specific context. For Notes/Domino users, this context is one of Notes for collaboration (email, calendaring, and instant messaging), an operating system with its file system for other work such as storage and retrieval of documents, and other applications and office technologies.

The IBM strategy for Notes/Domino is to allow the user, in his or her context, to collaborate more effectively in more and new flexible ways while maintaining the ability to support legacy and new open composite applications.

One way this is being done is by allowing developers new and better ways of taking complicated and related applications, and placing them together to create new conceptual whole applications, or composite applications (applications that are composed of two or more applications). In order to allow this within the Notes/Domino application platform, IBM has added new development tools and features, allowing Notes/Domino the ability to take part in the new world of Service Oriented Architectures (SOA, see Chapter 3) while continuing to support the rich legacy of applications already built.

Composite Applications

Composite applications are applications that consist of two or more components that may have been independently developed, working together to perform tasks that none of the member applications could perform by itself. Each component publishes and consumes messages from other components, and performs actions based upon user interaction or information received from other components. Support for composite applications is one of the central points for Notes/Domino 8. Composite applications in Notes 8 can wire together multiple components from Notes applications, Lotus Component Designer applications, and Eclipse into a single application context for the end user.

Composite applications, whether they are based on Notes/Domino 8, WebSphere Portal, or Lotus Expeditor, are the "front end" or user interface to an enterprise's SOA strategy. They, in effect, consume the services that are offered by the composite architectures put in place to support SOA.

An example of a composite application would be a simple customer relationship management application. This application needs to display a list of accounts, opportunities, and contacts to end users.

The accounts component should display accounts owned by the end user. When the end user selects an account in the account component, the opportunities for that account should be displayed in the opportunities component, and all of the contacts for the first opportunity should be displayed in the contacts component.

In the application described above, the components are "communicating" with each other by publishing and consuming properties via a property broker. When the user clicks on an account, the account component publishes the `accountkey` property to the property broker. The opportunities component has been written to "listen" for the `accountkey` property to be published, and when it is, it performs a lookup into a data store pulling back all the specific opportunities for the published account key. Once it has displayed all of the opportunities for the account, it selects the first opportunity for display and then publishes the `opportunitykey` property to the property broker. The contacts component then performs a lookup to display all of the contacts for the opportunity.

When the user selects a different opportunity, the opportunity component again publishes an `opportunitykey` property and the contacts component receives this new `opportunitykey` property and displays the correct contacts for the selected opportunity.

Using component applications, developers can respond quickly to requests from the line of business for functionality changes. For example, in the case of the customer relationship management application described above, the line of business may decide to purchase a telephony component to dial the phone and log all phone calls made. The developers of the application would need to simply modify the contact component to publish the phone number of a contact with a name that the new telephony component listens for and the call could be made on behalf of the user.

In addition to being used within the customer relationship management application, the components developed could be put together with other components to form entirely different applications. Each component already understands what data it needs to publish and consume to perform its actions, and contains the code to perform those specific actions on back-end systems. The reuse of the components will save the developers and the organization time each time whenever they are reused.

Composite applications also require a new programming model for Notes/Domino 8. This model mirrors the model within WebSphere Portal 6 in that multiple components are aggregated into a single UI with the property broker acting as the "glue" that allows the various components to interact and share data even if the components are from different systems. This programming model is something new in Notes 8 and required some changes to Domino Designer 8.

As a side note, the new programming model of composite applications will most probably bring its own set of problems. For example, what happens in a composite application when one of the components fails? In this "composite crash" situation, what does the composite application need to do in order to recover?

Additionally from an infrastructure point of view, composite applications will only be as available as their weakest component. What good would a reservations system implemented with many components be if one of the components were not hosted by a highly available infrastructure, while the others were? We see these sorts of issues being dealt with currently by customers venturing into the composite world via SOAs.

There are two main categories of change for development related to composite applications in Notes/Domino 8 application design and programming. We will look at both of them in the following sections.

Application Design

In order to allow your Notes or Domino application to participate within a composite application, you must first decide which design elements need to be accessible to other components. To make these components available to other components within your composite application, they are specified within a Web Services Description Language (WSDL) file. The composite application property broker then uses this WSDL file as a map into your application and its published properties and actions.

To allow this mapping to occur, the Composite Application Editor is used. Without making changes to legacy Notes/Domino application functionality, the Composite Application Editor can be used to surface the elements of the application such as forms, views, documents, and other Notes elements to the composite application.

Another element of composite application design is deciding where the application components will reside. Composite applications can be hosted within a local NSF file on a Notes client, on a Domino 8 application server, in WebSphere Portal, or in Lotus Expeditor. The Notes/Domino application components are created with the Composite Application Editor while WebSphere Portal composite applications can be created with the Composite Application Editor or the Portal Application Template Editor.

Programming

As mentioned previously, the addition of composite applications to the development strategy for Notes/Domino 8 required some changes and additions to the existing programming model.

Within a composite application, the components must be able to interact even if they were defined with different tools and technologies. Some components may even be stored within different database technologies. One component may be NSF based while another may be stored within a relational database store. The components need a standardized way to define the properties and actions that they support, so that an application developer can wire them together into a composite application. The standard way to define these properties and actions is via a WSDL file.

Let's take a quick look at properties, actions and wires.

Properties

Component properties are the data items that a given component produces. They are either input properties (consumed by the component) or output (produced by the component) properties. Each property is assigned a data type, which is based on the WC3 primitive data types. These include `string`, `Boolean`, `decimal`, `time`, and `date`. The primitive data types can also be utilized to build new data types. For example, within Notes 8, some new data types for components will be available that map to common data available within the mail, calendar, and contacts applications. Some of these new data types are listed in the following table:

Data Type Name	Extends Data Type	Description	Example
`mailTo`	`String`	List of people to receive an email	`"mailto:suzie@company.com?subject=Our Dogs are Smart&cc=frankie@company.com,domino@company.com&bcc=gromit@company.com`

`emailAddress822`	`String`	Email address following RFC 822	`"My Gerbil <shelbie@company.com>"`
			
			 `"Little Man <nate@company.com>"`

`distinguishedName`	`String`	LDAP name	`"cn=bubbles,ou=turtles,dc=company,dc=com"`

Actions

Actions are the logic that is used to consume a property. For example, a component may implement an action that sends an email when it receives a `mailTo` type property from another component. The code within the component that sends the email based on the information consumed from the property is the action for the component. Components can obviously contain multiple actions depending on the business logic required for the component.

It is easy to confuse a web services action with a Notes action. The web services action is a name in a WSDL file that represents functionality that will consume a property. Notes actions can be coupled with a web services action so that the Notes action gets called to consume a property. The LotusScript in the Notes action can then implement code to act on the property.

The illustration below shows a Notes action in the Notes 8 mail template that is coupled with a web services action `NewMemoUsingMailtoURL`. You can see that in the code, the LotusScript is using a property broker to gain access to the property.

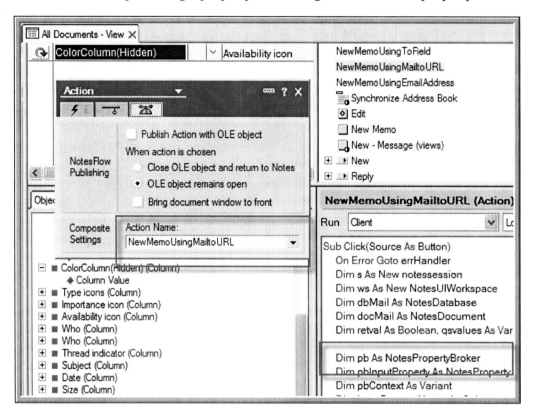

Wires

Wires are the construct by which components interact within a composite application. A wire is simply a programmatic definition of which components talk to each other. The components must share common properties and then produce and consume them via actions. More simply put, wires connect properties to actions.

For example, an application developer could wire together a contact list component with an email component. When the user selects a contact from the contact list, the contact list component would produce and publish a `mailTo` type property, which could then be consumed by the email component. The email component would consume the published `mailTo` property and compose an email using the data contained within the property.

The following shows the components available within the Notes 8 mail template that are available for use in other component applications as well, shown from the component palette within the new Composite Application Editor.

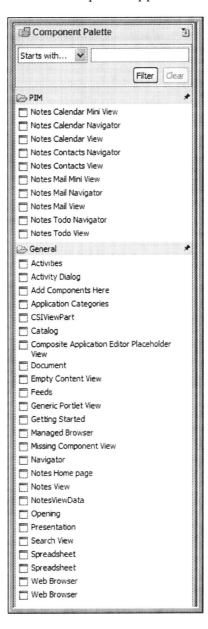

New Features in Domino Designer 8

With the addition of composite applications to the development strategy of Notes/ Domino 8, there are a number of changes required to Domino Designer 8 to allow for composite applications design, development, and use. Some additional new tools were also required.

These changes augment existing functionality. They were made without sacrificing supportability of existing applications. They allow legacy applications as well as new applications to play a part in an SOA by providing a platform that permits multiple technologies to be combined into a single application, side by side.

Composite Applications Support

New Domino Designer 8 features that support composite applications include the Property Broker Editor and the Composite Application Editor.

Property Broker Editor

One of the first things you will notice in Domino Designer 8 is the new support for composite application design elements. These design elements store the WSDL and XML files for wiring properties and applications. You can see these new design elements by selecting the **Composite Applications** item in the view.

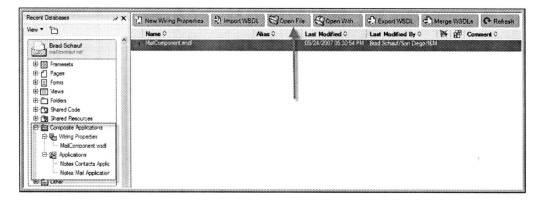

The **Wiring Properties** view is where Domino Designer stores the WSDL that defines the properties, types and actions for the application. These design elements are edited with the Property Broker Editor, which is new in Domino Designer 8. To edit wiring properties, select the wiring property from the new Notes 8 mail template and click the **Open File** button. This will bring up the Property Broker Editor. The Property Broker Editor allows you to create or edit the properties, types or actions for your applications. Once the Property Broker Editor has saved the WSDL as a design element, you will be able to associate the defined properties and actions with other design elements.

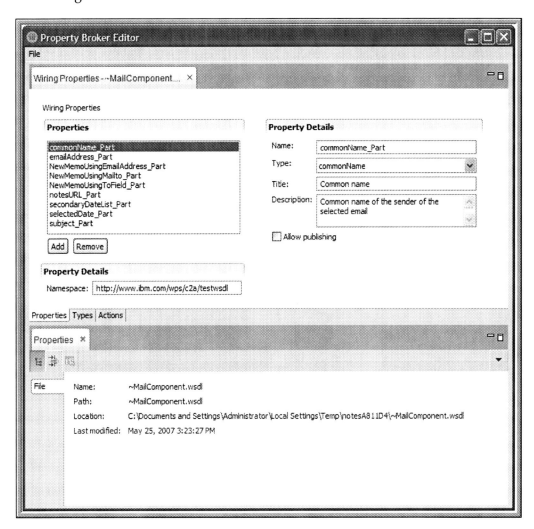

Composite Application Editor

Also within the **Composite Applications** view within Domino Designer 8, is the **Applications** listing. These design elements store the XML that define the makeup of the composite applications and their associated wiring.

Launching the Composite Application Editor is not done via the Domino Designer interface however, and may confuse new composite application developers. To launch the Composite Application Editor, open Notes and then select **Action | Edit Application**.

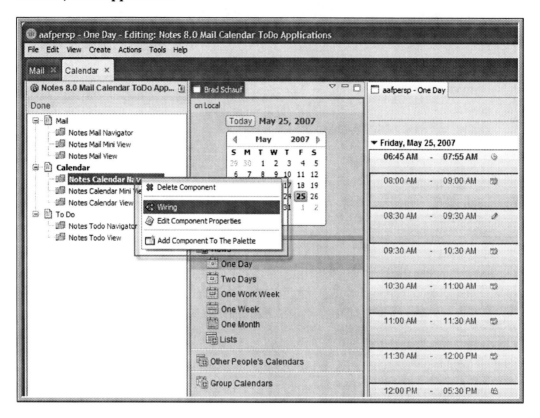

Once the Composite Application Editor is open, you can select a component and then edit the wires for this component.

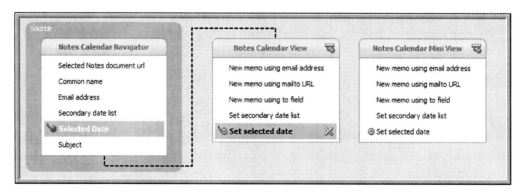

The illustration above shows the wiring properties for the Notes Calendar Navigator component.

Web Services Consumer

Web services were supported starting with Notes/Domino 7. However, the web services supported with Domino 7 could only be web service providers. They could be called as a normal web service from a remote computer and return information from Domino databases, or perform other Domino-related functions. It was also possible in release 7 to write web service consumers and have them hosted by Domino, but there was no specific support for web service consumers within Domino and creating them was a matter of Java development.

With the release of Notes and Domino 8, Domino-based web service consumers are supported. Notes/Domino applications can now call web services hosted on remote computers. Notes/Domino 8 makes it simple to call web services. Domino Designer will even import the WSDL and create the code required to use the web service for you.

Unlike web service providers in Domino, which are stored in special design elements, web service consumers in Domino 8 are stored in a special type of script library. This script library can be written in either Java or LotusScript. Just as with other script libraries, code that wants to use the web service consumer must use the script library that contains it.

Consuming a web service in Notes/Domino 8 is very simple. The high level steps are:

1. Locate a web service that you would like to consume and acquire its WSDL file.
2. Create a new script library to contain the web service consumer.
3. Import the WSDL file into the new script library.
4. Have your application call the script library so as to consume the web service.

For this example, we have selected a free stock quote web service that retrieves 20 minute delayed quotes from Yahoo. The web service description and its WSDL file are located here:

```
http://www.webservicelist.com/webservices/f.asp?fid=37722
```

We will create a script library to contain the web service, create a form with a simple button to prompt the user for a company symbol, and then call or consume the web service and display the resultant stock quote.

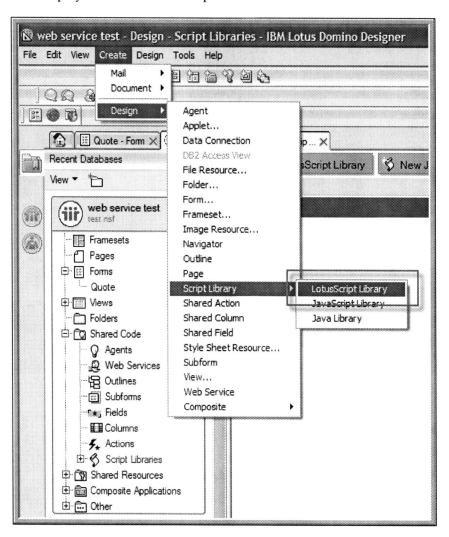

Once you have selected a web service to consume and have its WSDL file, you need to create a new script library to contain the web service code. Create a new application, and select **Create | Design | Script Library**. Select either LotusScript Library or Java Library depending on your language of choice. For this example, we will create a LotusScript library. Save the script library and provide a name for it when prompted. For this example, we called the script library stockquote. Keep this script library open.

You now have a new, empty script library. At the bottom of the code window in Domino Designer, you will see a button labeled **WSDL**. This button will allow you to import the WSDL file that describes the web service that you are going to consume and also generate the code for consuming this web service. This will save you a lot of time going through the WSDL file and crafting your classes!

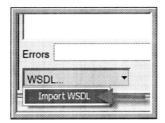

Import the WSDL file that you downloaded for your selected service. Notice that Domino Designer generates the class required to consume the web service.

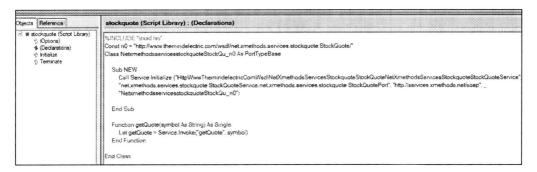

For the free stock quote service selected, the generated LotusScript code look like this:

```
Option Declare
%INCLUDE "lsxsd.lss"
Const n0 = "http://www.themindelectric.com/wsdl/net.xmethods.services.
stockquote.StockQuote/"
Class Netxmethodsservicesstockquote StockQu_n0 As PortTypeBase
```

```
Sub NEW
        Call Service.Initialize
("HttpWwwThemindelectricComWsdlNetXmethodsServicesStockquoteStockQuo
teNetXmethodsServicesStockquoteStockQuoteService",_
"net.xmethods.services.stockquote.StockQuoteService.net.xmethods.
services.stockquote.StockQuotePort", "http://services.xmethods.net/
soap", _ "NetxmethodsservicesstockquoteStockQu_n0"
End Sub


    Function getQuote(symbol As String) As Single
        Let getQuote = Service.Invoke("getQuote", symbol)
    End Function


End Class
```

Notice that Domino Designer did the hard work of decoding the WSDL file to create a class with functions to consume the web service. If you like, you may even decide to modify the generated code so as to make it a bit more readable – by changing the class name, for example.

It is a good idea at this time to inspect the code that was generated and become familiar with it. In this example, we can see the generated LotusScript created a class called etxmethodsservicesstockquoteStockQu_n0 and a function called getQuote. Domino Designer got these values from the WSDL file that was imported. We will use the class name and the function name later within our button that will call the script library that consumes the web service.

Now, all we need is some code to consume the web service via the special web services enabled script library that we just created. To keep things simple, let's create a button on a form that will prompt the user for a stock symbol and then display the results.

Create a blank form. Within the Globals section of the form, place the following code, which disallows implicit variable declarations (a good practice) and identifies the script library stockquote as used within the form:

```
Option Public
Use "stockquote"
```

On the same form, create a new button. Give the button a clever label like **Get a stock quote**, and then insert the following code into the button:

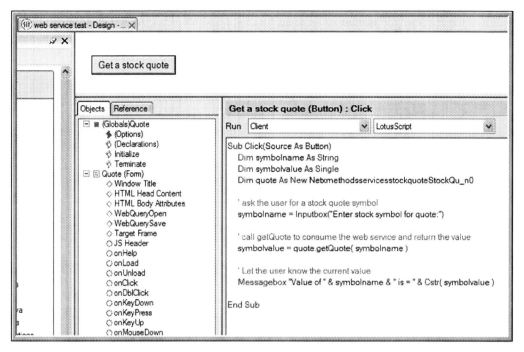

```
Dim symbolname As String
Dim symbolvalue As Single
Dim quote As New NetxmethodsservicesstockquoteStockQu_n0

' ask the user for a stock quote symbol
symbolname = Inputbox("Enter stock symbol for quote:")

' call getQuote to consume the web service and return the value
symbolvalue = quote.getQuote( symbolname )

' Let the user know the current value
Messagebox "Value of " & symbolname & " is = " & Cstr( symbolvalue )
```

Save the form, and then open the application. Create a new instance of the form that contains the button.

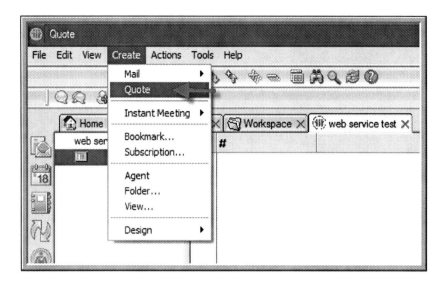

Now click on the button to invoke the code within it. You will be prompted to enter the stock symbol whose quote you would like to retrieve via the web service. For this example, we selected my favorite hamburger chain.

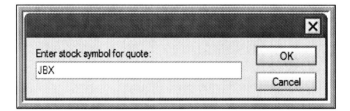

When you click on **OK**, Notes will execute the code so as to invoke and consume the web service. Once that has been done, Notes will then process the `Messagebox` call so as to present the results.

This is obviously a very simple example of consuming a web service, but it should open your mind to the possibilities. There are web services available for almost anything you can imagine. Some are free and others are for a fee. You can use web services to retrieve grocery items by UPC number, perform credit card transaction processing, and even track packages shipped with FedEx or UPS.

Now that Notes/Domino 8 can consume web services, you have another data integration tool at your disposal.

Domino IBM DB/2 Integration

The ability to use DB/2 as an alternate back-end storage system for Domino was available in Domino 7 as a Feature Trial and also via a Limited Availability program. With the release of Notes/Domino 8, the integration with DB 2 will be generally available on certain Windows, IBM AIX, and Linux operating systems.

Using this integration, you can make data within your Domino databases available for use by relational database tools and show external relational data within Notes/Domino views and embedded views.

View Enhancements

Domino Designer 8 view enhancements include new column number formats, extended to use available window width, defer index creation until first use, and show default items in right-mouse menu.

New Column Number Format

There is a new number format for number columns that will display the column contents in kilobytes, megabytes, or gigabytes, which makes it much easier to determine the relative size of the number represented in the column. In this example, the size of file attachments is used.

When displayed in Notes 7, the column shows just the attachments lengths for each document.

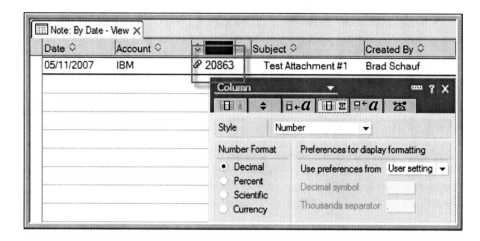

However, when the same column is displayed in Notes 8 with the Bytes (K/M/G) number format, the column displays a much friendlier format.

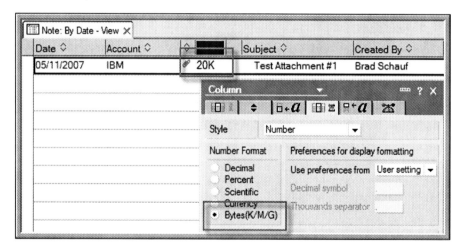

Extend to Use Available Window Width

In Notes 8, you can select which column within a view will expand to utilize the available width of the window. In previous releases, this option was only available for the last column in a view.

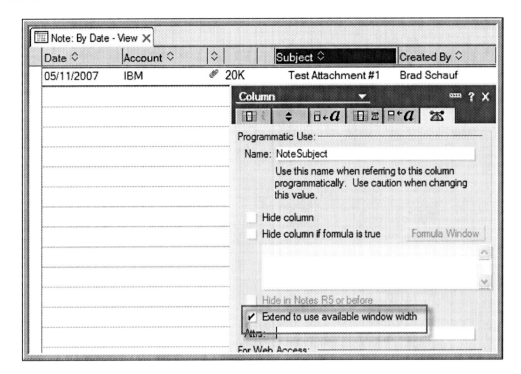

 For this option to work, the view level option **Extend last column to window width** takes precedence and must be deselected. In addition, the column to be extended must be marked as **Resizable**. Multiple columns can be designated to extend to use the available window width. However, only the first column, which has this attribute set, will expand.

Defer Index Creation until First Use

Index creation can now be deferred for **Click on column header to sort** view columns. Using this option, the view index won't be created until a user first clicks on the column to sort it. Only views that users click to sort will have their indexes built. This can help reduce the load on servers, as not all column indexes will be created automatically. They will only be created when they are used.

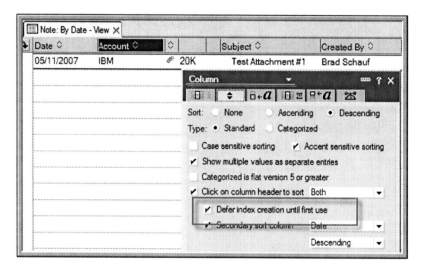

Note that the deferred index creation feature requires the database to be using the new ODS (On-Disk Structure) for Notes/Domino 8. By default, Notes/Domino 8 still creates databases with ODS 43, which was introduced in release 6 and used through releases 7 and 8. To enable the creation of databases in ODS 48 format, use the `Create_R8_Databases=1 Notes.ini` parameter on the Domino 8 server or the Notes 8 client.

Show Default Items in Right-Mouse Menu

Developers have been able to add custom actions to the right-mouse menu with previous versions of Notes/Domino. With release 8, you can choose not to have the default right-mouse menu items shown in the menu, allowing just the menu items you select to be displayed.

The default is to show just default items. The picture above shows that we have deselected the option allowing only the actions that we select to be shown in the menu. This will make it easier for the end user of the application to find the actions we have defined for the view or folder.

Form Enhancements

There is a new rich text lite field option that allows you to add a thumbnail picture to a form. This new feature is used in the Notes/Domino 8 address book templates.

For example, in the personal address book template, you can add pictures of your contacts to their contact records. This is handy to help remember the face that goes with the name.

To add the thumbnail picture to a contact note in Notes 8, edit the contact record, click on the import icon, and select the picture.

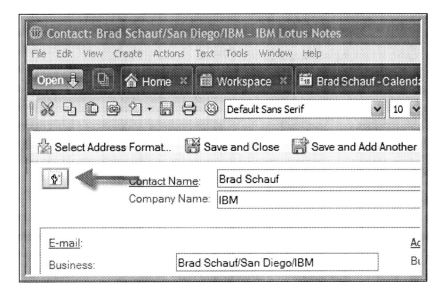

Once the picture has been selected, it will be displayed in place of the import button.

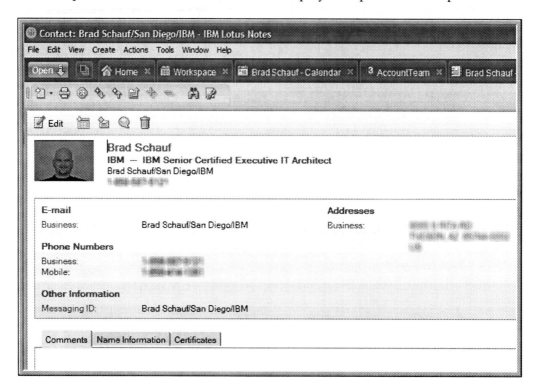

To delete the picture, you should edit the document, select the thumbnail, and press the delete key.

To enable thumbnails in your rich text lite field, select the second tab of the properties box, and then select **Thumbnail** in the **Only allow** selection field. When **Thumbnail** is selected, all of the other options will automatically be deselected for you. Also, you may only select **Thumbnail** in the **First Display** property.

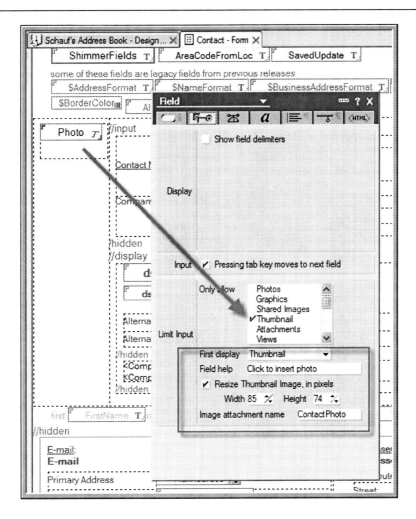

You can also have Notes resize the thumbnail image by selecting the width and height in pixels.

Agent Enhancements

Agents can now be tagged so as to determine when the server starts. These agents will start the server a few minutes after the Domino server boots up. They should not be relied upon to start immediately.

Agents triggered to start when the server starts will not run when just the agent manager itself is restarted. They will only run when the entire Domino server is started. This allows agents to perform actions that should only occur after a server has started and not be repeated each time agent manager starts up.

To trigger an agent this way, select **When Server Starts** for the **On event** trigger type.

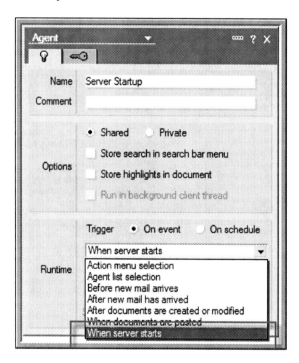

Agents that are triggered when the server starts can also be given dates to start and stop running. This could be helpful if the agent is implementing a date driven business process.

To edit these agents' schedule properties, click the **Edit Settings** button on the **Agent** properties box.

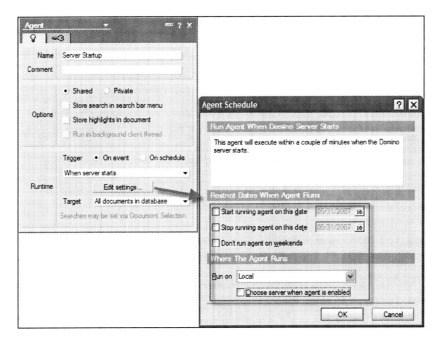

Formula Language and LotusScript Additions

Domino Designer 8 includes several enhancements to formula language and LotusScript.

Formula Language Additions

The following are some selected new commands that are available within Notes/Domino 8.

@Command([CopySelectedAsTable]): This new command performs the same action as its menu command counterpart, **Edit | Copy As | Table**, which copies one or more selected view entries into a table. It places the table of the selected view entries on the clipboard. It also includes a link to each of the documents in the table. This is very useful when sending co-workers links to documents from a database in a pre-formatted table.

@Command([OpenInNewWindow]): This new command allows your formula language code to open a document from a view, folder, or calendar in a new window instead of opening it within a new tab within Lotus Notes.

LotusScript Additions

The following are some selected new classes, methods, and events available within Notes/Domino 8. The NotesProperty and NotesProperyBroker classes, and the Onselect event were added to support the new composite application-programming model.

`MarkAllRead` and `MarkAllUnread` methods: Finally, within the `NotesView`, `NotesViewEntryCollection`, and `NotesViewNavigator` classes, two new methods dealing with read/unread marks are available. Using these classes, you can mark documents as having been read or unread using the `MarkAllRead` or `MarkAllUnread` methods. These methods will affect the documents within the collection or navigator. There are, of course, Java counterparts available.

`NotesDirectory` class: Objects created with this new class correspond to the directories on a specific Domino server or Notes client. The objects are contained within a `NotesSession` object, and they contains one or more `NotesDirectoryNavigator` objects. The following properties are available in the `NotesDirectory` class. Unless otherwise specified, these properties are read-only.

Property	Type	Description
AvailableItems	Variant array	This property is set by the methods LookupNames and LookupAllNames. If a NotesDirectory object has been created but no lookups have been performed with it, this property will be null.
AvailableNames	Variant array	This property will contain the names returned from the most recent LookupAllNames or LookupNames call. If a NotesDirectory object has been created but no lookups have been performed with it, this property will be null.
AvailableView	String	This property contains the name of the view specified in the most recent LookupAllNames or LookupNames call. If a NotesDirectory object has been created but no lookups have been performed with it, this property will be null.
GroupAuthorizationOnly	Boolean	Read/write property. This property controls which directories will be used during lookups. If the property is True, only directories marked "Enable for Group Authorization" will be searched. If set to False, the default, lookups performed will search all directories available.

Property	Type	Description
LimitMatches	Boolean	Read/write property. If `True`, directory lookups will be limited to fifty entries. If `False` then lookups performed will return all matches.
PartialMatches	Boolean	Controls whether or not lookups will match on partial names. If `True`, partial names will match. If `False`, the default, lookups will not match on partial names.
SearchAllDirectories	Boolean	Read/write property. If `True`, the default, all directories will be searched during lookups. If `False`, lookups will cease after the first directory containing the view name specified.
Server	String	This property contains the name of the server represented by the instance of `NotesDirectory`.
TrustedOnly	Boolean	Read/write property. This property controls which directories will be used during lookups. If `True`, lookups will search only directories which contain trust information. If `False`, the default, the lookups will search all directories.
UseContextServer	Boolean	Read/write property. This property controls whether the server of the context database or the server specified in the lookup methods will be used. If True, the server context database will be used. If `False`, the default, and then the server specified in the lookup method will be used.

The following methods are available for the `NotesDirectory` class.

Method	Returns	Description
CreateNavigator	NotesDirectoryNavigator	Use to create additional `DirectoryNavigators` to allow multiple `DirectoryNavigators` to be used.
FreeLookupBuffer	N/A	Since the resultant name lookup buffers can be quite large, this method can be used to free memory in the current lookup buffer, in effect resetting all navigators. Used for memory management.

Method	Returns	Description
LookupAllNames	NotesDirectoryNavigator	Performs a lookup of designated items contained within the specified view.
LookupNames	NotesDirectoryNavigator	Performs a lookup of designated items contained within the specified view for the specified items.

NotesDirectoryNavigator class: NotesDirectoryNavigator objects are returned by methods of the NotesDirectory class and allow the developer to navigate the items returned by a directory search. The following properties are available for the NotesDirectoryNavigator class. Unless otherwise specified, these properties are read-only.

Property	Type	Description
CurrentItem	String	This property will contain the current item for the NotesDirectoryNavigator and is updated with subsequent calls of GetNextItemValue and GetNthItemValue methods.
CurrentMatch	Long	An index to the current match for the NotesDirectoryNavigator and is updated by subsequent calls to FindFirstMatch, FindNextMatch and FindNthMatch methods.
CurrentName	String	The name of the current match indicated by the CurrentMatch property index for NotesDirectoryNavigators created with the LookupNames method.
CurrentView	String	Contains the name of the directory view used to create the NotesDirectoryNavigator object. This property is updated when directory lookups are performed.
MatchLocated	Boolean	If True, a match was successful. If False, the match was not successful.
NameLocated	Boolean	If True, a name was located. If False, the name was not located.

The following methods are available for the `NotesDirectoryNavigator` class.

Method	Returns	Description
FindFirstMatch	Boolean	Moves the navigator of the first match of the current name in the `NotesDirectoryNavigator`. Returns `True` if a match was found otherwise returns `False` indicating no match was found.
FindNextMatch	Boolean	Moves the navigator of the next match of the current name in the `NotesDirectoryNavigator`. Returns `True` if a match was found otherwise returns `False` indicating no match was found.
FindNthMatch	Boolean	Moves the navigator of the nth match of the current name in the `NotesDirectoryNavigator`. Returns `True` if a match was found, otherwise returns `False` indicating no match was found.
FindFirstName	Long	Moves the navigator to the first name in the `NotesDirectoryNavigator` returning the number of matches found.
FindNextName	Long	Moves the navigator to the next name in the `NotesDirectoryNavigator` returning the number of matches found.
FindNthName	Long	Moves the navigator to the nth name in the `NotesDirectoryNavigator` returning the number of matches found.
GetFirstItemValue	Variant	Returns the value of the first item of the current match.
GetNextItemValue	Variant	Moves the navigator to the next item within the current match and returns the value of that match.
GetNthItemValue	Variant	Moves the navigator to the nth item within the current match and returns the value of that match.

`NotesProperty class:` This class represents a single component property within the composite application. Component properties are data items that a given component produces and the `NotesProperty` class allows your application to manage the publishing of the defined properties within an application.

The methods for the NotesProperty class are only active when used within the Notes 8 Standard configuration. They are not available when used by applications running on Domino server or from within the Notes 8 Basic configuration.

The following properties are available for the NotesProperty class. Unless otherwise specified, the properties are read-only.

Property	Type	Description
Description	String	This class property returns the description for the NotesProperty object.
IsInput	Boolean	If True, the property is an input property. If False, the property is an output property.
Name	String	This class property returns the name of the NotesProperty.
NameSpace	String	This class property returns the namespace for the NotesProperties data-type.
Title	String	This class property returns the title of the NotesProperty.
TypeName	String	This class property returns the type name of the NotesProperty. When combined with the NameSpace property, it provides a unique identifier for the NotesProperty type.
Values	Variant array of Strings, Integer, Real, or NotesDateTime	This read/write class property sets or returns the array of values for the NotesProperty. The array items must be of all the same data type and input properties by definition cannot be set using this property. The Publish method must be called after using this property to set values or the values will not persist.

The following methods are available for the NotesProperty class.

Method	Returns	Description
Clear	N/A	For output properties only, this method clears the new or modified values of the specified property from the temporary cache used for publishing via the property broker. If called from an input type NotesProperty the method will have no effect.
Publish	N/A	Publishes to the property broker the new values for the NotesPropery object.

`NotesPropertyBroker` **class**: The following properties are available for the `NotesPropertyBroker` class. This is where all the composite application magic occurs in Notes/Domino 8.

The current implementation of the property broker for Notes/Domino 8 only supports a single input property. The `InputPropertyContext` is, however, declared as an array to allow for future expansion of the property broker to support multiple input properties in the future.

Unless otherwise specified, the properties are read-only.

Property	Type	Description
`InputPropertyContext`	`Array of NotesProperty`	Returns an array of `NotesProperty` objects, with only the first item of the array populated.

The methods for the `NotesPropertyBroker` class are only active when used within the Notes 8 Standard configuration. They are not available when used by applications running on Domino server or from within the Notes 8 Basic configuration.

The following methods are available for the NotesPropertyBroker class.

Method	Returns	Description
`ClearProperty`	N/A	Clears the new or modified values of a specified property from the temporary cache used for publishing.
`GetProperty`	`NotesProperty`	Returns a `NotesPropery` object for a specified property.
`GetPropertyValue`	`Variant` array of **Strings**, `Integer`, `Real`, or `NotesDateTime`	Returns the value of a specified input property. Used when implementing an action.
`HasProperty`	`Boolean`	If `True`, the specified property is associated with the property broker. If `False`, the property broker does not have a property with the specified name.
`Publish`	N/A	If values of the `NotesPropertyBroker` have been modified, this method will publish them
`SetPropertyValue`	`NotesProperty`	Returns a `NotesProperty` object with the value of a specified output property.

Onselect event: This new event was added to the NotesUIView class to give developers the trigger needed to have other components respond to selected documents within a view. The Onselect event is used to contain code that publishes properties to the property broker based on the documents selected.

What's Ahead?

As you know, Domino Designer is used to create Notes/Domino applications. You have seen how it can be used to take a Notes application and build components from the various Notes/Domino design elements using the Property Broker Editor and the Composite Application Editor, and new integration points with actions and view columns.

Future plans for Domino Designer may include merging it with Lotus Component Designer within an Eclipse framework, bringing the two designer tools together into an integrated development framework for Lotus applications. All development will be performed within the Eclipse environment with new script editors and shared design element bookmark navigation.

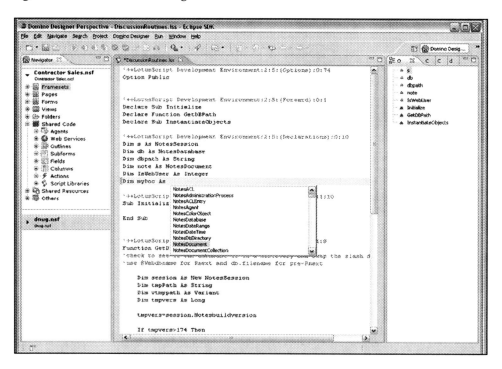

Bringing these multiple development tools under a single designer framework will make the developer's job easier by offering them a consolidated view of the development process.

Lotus Component Designer

Lotus Component Designer is the new version of Workplace Designer, with support for WebSphere Portal 6. It is a development environment built on top of Eclipse, which allows for the creation of document based applications using visual design methods with no need to know the intricacies of J2EE.

Forms are the building blocks for applications built with Lotus Component Design. Applications can have more than one form associated with them. Each form then contains one or more controls. Controls include things like views, images, text boxes, combo boxes, radio buttons, and tables.

Once controls are placed on a form, the built-in JavaScript editor can be used to customize functionality. The JavaScript editor supports color-coding and code-assist, so developers who are comfortable developing in Domino Designer will feel right at home.

The forms and controls within a Lotus Component Designer application are used to manipulate an XML-based document model, which is stored in a relational database. This allows for the separation of the look and feel of the application from its data.

Here are some selected new features of Lotus Component Designer.

Migration Tool

Lotus Component Designer allows you to migrate components created with previous releases into release 8. The migration tool is a part of the component import process and can detect older versions of components. When an older version is detected, its pages are converted to the new XSP format.

Help and Enhanced Welcome Page

The new Lotus Component Designer welcome page offers a rich set of options including an overview, tutorials, samples, Web resources, and context-sensitive help.

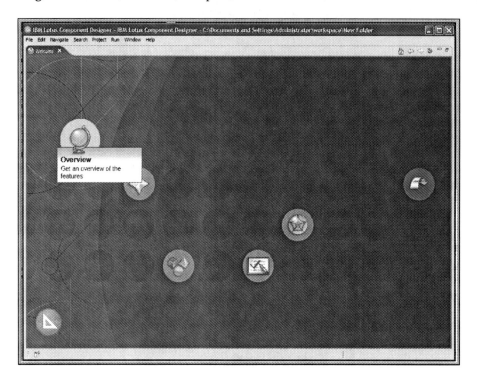

Accessibility

Lotus Component Designer is an accessible software development tool with which you can create accessible components. It is compliant with IBM Corporate Instruction 162 (CI 162) which meets the U.S. government federal accessibility guidelines for information technology. It requires that hardware, software, services, web pages, and internal applications are accessible to persons with disabilities.

Composite Application Support

With Lotus Component Designer, you can now create applications that can work within the IBM WebSphere Portal composite application model. These components can interact with components created with Notes/Domino 8 as well.

Controls and Pages

There are many new features and additions to controls and pages. Here are a few favorites:

- Preview images directly from the **Choose Image** dialog box without having to add it to the page first.
- Create custom controls, which combine two or more controls into a single control.
- Add UI controls that are not listed in the standard UI Controls palette, such as supported AJAX controls.
- Web page preview without having to leave Lotus Component Designer.

Data Connections

Some of the new features and enhancements for data connectivity are the following:

- Local connections are supported in components. Connections are the sets of information used to connect to a data source such as a database.
- The schema editor has been improved so as to provide an easy graphical way to create and edit XML schemas.
- Components can now store data in external data sources such as Domino databases and XML files on a target server
- A new query editor is available to provide a more granular and flexible way to populate view queries.
- Components can now consume external web services and manipulate the data received with JavaScript

Scripting

Some of the new features and enhancements for deployment are the following:

- There is a new XSP file format for registry and page loading which has been made public. For more information, visit the Lotus Component Designer developerWorks web site at `http://www.ibm.com/software/workplace/products/product5.nsf/wdocs/workplacedesigner`
- A new XSP tag library is available offering a library of UI controls, data sources, simple actions and other controls. This library is located in the `\doc\controls` directory.
- A JavaScript debugger is now included and can be used to debug any JavaScript code that runs on WebSphere Portal 6.x.

Deployment

Some of the new features and enhancements for deployment are:

- Components can be deployed to servers without knowledge of J2EE applications and without the administrator credentials.

- Components can be deployed to a cluster for production deployment by exporting the components WAR (Web ARchive) and DDL (Data Definition Language) files and providing them to you administrators.

- Basic authentication is now supported for WebSphere Portal 6.x

New Web 2.0 Features

The following are some of the new Web 2.0 features that are available in Notes/ Domino 8.

RSS and ATOM

RSS and ATOM are feed formats used to publish web content that is updated on a regular basis. News organizations, governments, private companies, and even individuals via their daily blogs publish RSS and ATOM feeds. All you need to read these feeds is an RSS or ATOM reader such as Notes 8 and access to the Internet.

Feeds within Lotus Notes 8 are included as a side bar plug-in along with the **Sametime Contacts**, **Activities**, and **Day at a Glance**, on the right side of the screen.

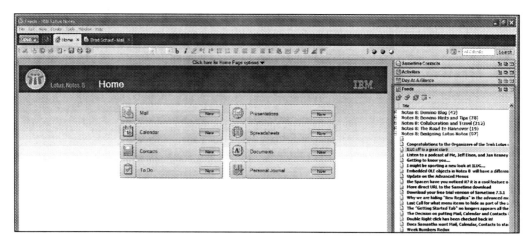

With Notes/Domino 8, you can also generate RSS feeds from Domino databases including the new blog template and Domino Web Access. The Domino RSS Syndication template is used to create the feeds from any Domino view. The agents and script libraries from this template can also be used within other applications.

The first step is to create a database to manage your feeds. Create the new application and base it on the RSS Feed Generator template.

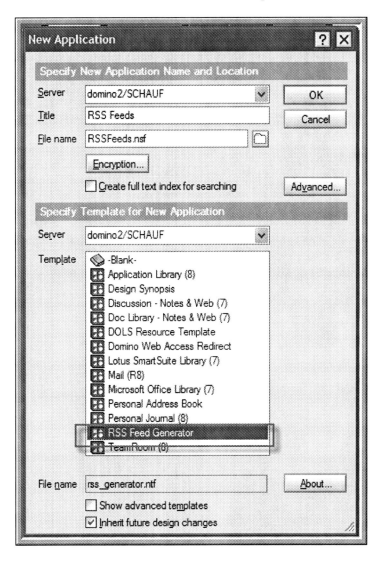

Once the database has been created, you will want to set up the global options that apply to all the RSS feeds that are generated. To do this, click **Set Global Options** in the action bar of the application.

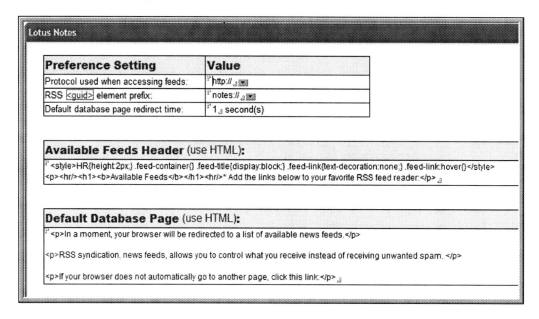

Using the **Global options** dialog, you can control the following:

- The protocol for accessing feeds – either HTTP or HTTPS.
- The RSS `<guid>` element prefix – either `notes://` or `http://`.
- The default database redirect time, entered in seconds.
- The available feeds header, via HTML.
- The default HTML for the feed database, via HTML.

Once the defaults are set, you can define a feed and direct it to a specific mail file, based on a user or on a specific database.

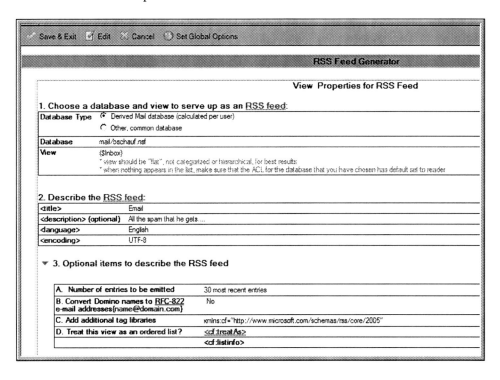

With a feed defined, you are able to get a listing of all available feeds from the Domino server by directing your browser to the feed database that you created earlier. From this web page, you will be able to add the feed into your favorite RSS feed reader.

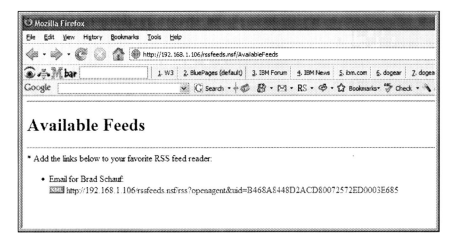

Blog Template

With Notes 8 you can create your own web log, or blog, using the new Domino Web
Log template (`dominoblog.ntf`). Once created, you can use either Notes:

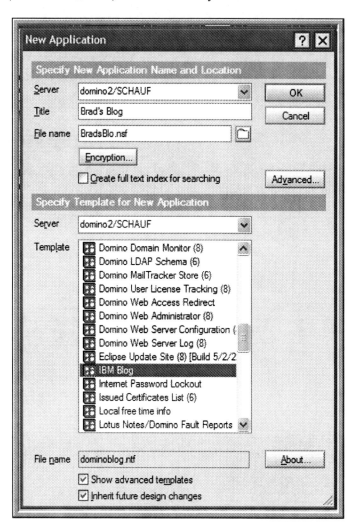

…or a web browser:

…to add content and manage your blog. The resultant web page shows the first entry of the author's blog. The template allows creation of blog entries from the Notes client or from the web site itself.

AJAX Support

Domino 8 adds support for JavaScript Object Notation (JSON) as an output format.

Lotus Expeditor

Lotus Expeditor is the base platform for Lotus rich clients such as Notes 8 Standard and Sametime 7.5. It is also a product that companies can leverage to build their own rich client solutions. Built on top of Eclipse (an open source IDE), Lotus Expeditor adds the ability to create composite applications, a local data store for credentials and application data, role based provisioning, enhanced security, and offline abilities.

One of the problems with rich clients in the past was the cost of deployment and support. Rich clients are large installations that needed to be upgraded and supported. In fact, it is the cost of deployment and support that helped to drive the web based applications that we see in wide use today. Everyone with a rich client knew what version of it they were running, but there is no reason to know what version of eBay, Google Mail, or your corporate WebSphere Portal you may be using because they are server managed and was updated all the time with new features, functions, and content.

In fact as the rush towards web-based applications required more and more functionality to be supported by the browser, the "light browser" itself became very large and started to require deployment and support planning. In some instances the browser footprint on a client became larger than some rich client applications.

Lotus Expeditor can be thought of as a platform that has all the benefits of rich clients but also has the benefits of those web-based applications because it can be centrally managed. It can also been described as a "local portal" because it can be used to create composite applications that contain Notes/Domino 8 components, JSR -168 compliant portlets, SWING, and AWT applications without the need for a network connection.

Lotus Expeditor does this by implementing client side containers for the components that communicate via a local property broker implementation. This can have another benefit – speed of execution. Since the code is executing within the Lotus Expeditor platform, the composite application may not be affected by network and back-end systems latency or at least only to the extent that it utilizes those systems.

In addition to responsiveness, applications built with Lotus Expeditor can also be more reliable and portable due to their local execution and data stores. This results in a rich client that has the benefits of a browser but with a user experience that can be better than a browser due to speed, reliability, centralized management, and the ability to work online or offline. When working offline, the applications store transactions in the local data store. Once connected to the company network, Lotus Expeditor can then synchronize the transactions to the host application and may even download updates for the application itself.

Some of the applications Lotus customers can build with Lotus Expeditor include customer service and support application such as bank teller and reservations clerk, as well as sales force automation applications such as mobile CRM or insurance claims management.

Summary

In this chapter, we reviewed some of the major new features and enhancements that affect Notes/Domino 8 application development. These included enhancements related to composite applications, Domino Designer 8, formula language and LotusScript, Lotus Component Designer, Web 2.0, and Lotus Expeditor.

10
Integration with Other Lotus/ IBM Products

The Lotus brand within IBM Software group represents the "people facing" side of the overall IBM product family. This does not necessarily mean the end user uses no other IBM products, but the Lotus brand is the front end of the IBM SOA Interaction Services component.

The following diagram shows the interaction between these components. Each can be deployed as a separate infrastructure piece and provide value. However, when they are leveraged as an integrated solution, the possibilities are nearly endless.

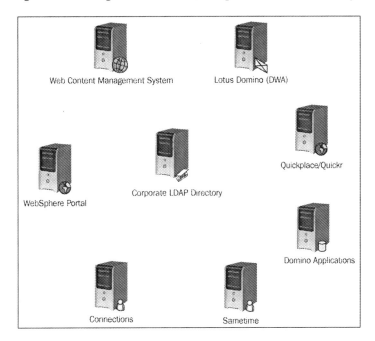

WebSphere Portal Server provides an on-the-glass integration solution for your enterprise. It allows you to create composite role-based applications from different data sources. For more information, see `http://www.ibm.com/websphere/portal`.

Web Content Management is now an integrated piece of the WebSphere Portal Server. It provides an end user driven content authoring and content delivery system. See `http://www.ibm.com/websphere/portal`.

Lotus Notes/Domino is IBM's flagship messaging and collaboration product, deployed to over 100 million users. It provides a foundation on which many of the other value-added products build. See `http://www.ibm.com/software/sw-lotus/products/product4.nsf/wdocs/dominohomepage`.

Lotus Quickplace/Quickr is IBM's team collaboration product. It provides template-based services and a set of content connectors, allowing end users to quickly create interactive team places, all without the need for administrator intervention. See `http://www.ibm.com/software/sw-lotus/products/product3.nsf/wdocs/ltwhome`.

Lotus Sametime is IBM's unified communications and collaboration product. It provides enterprise-class instant messaging and web conferencing services, as well as a platform for many other capabilities. This includes telephony and voice integration services. See `http://www.ibm.com/software/sw-lotus/products/product3.nsf/wdocs/st75home`.

Lotus Connections is IBM's "social networking" product. It provides a new category of integrated application services covering the following areas: activities, dogear, blogs, communities, and profiles. See `http://www.ibm.com/software/sw-lotus/products/product3.nsf/wdocs/connections`.

This chapter discusses add-on products for a typical Notes/Domino infrastructure. The specific products covered in this chapter are the most common, and they include:

- Lotus Quickplace/Quickr
- Lotus Sametime
- Lotus Connections

Each of these represents key components in the overall product strategy IBM has for the collaboration space.

This chapter does not cover all the products available under the Lotus brand. For additional information on these, visit `http://www.lotus.com`.

Lotus Quickplace/Quickr

The Lotus Quickplace product has been available for several years. Quickplace has become recognized as a leader in web-based team collaboration, and it is used in many large corporations throughout the world.

In early 2007, IBM announced two important changes to the Quickplace product family:

- The new version of Lotus Quickplace will be renamed Lotus Quickr.

- A new J2EE based version of Quickplace will be introduced, also called Lotus Quickr.

These two versions of Quickr (one based on Domino and one based on WebSphere Portal) form a single product. They do, however, have very different deployment architectures. From an end user's standpoint, they should be viewed as collaboration appliances. They will be presented with a consolidated list of places where they are involved so that they can easily navigate. This will be the case regardless of the backend deployment architecture.

The goal of these changes to Quickplace/Quickr is simplification. IBM wants the product to be so simple that an end user can, with a few clicks, generate productive services. There is also a focus on server deployment simplification. This will be covered in detail later in this chapter.

One of the key components of Quickr is the connector technology that it introduces. These connectors will allow for direct and programmatic interaction with the data stored in the Quickr places. Connectors that will be shipping with Quickr 8.0 are the following:

- Notes
- Sametime
- File System/Windows Explorer
- RSS/ATOM

In this section, we will cover each edition and discuss how it integrates with Domino. We will not be covering how to install the product itself; this is covered in detail within the product documentation.

Quickr with Services for Domino

The Domino-based edition of Quickr should be thought of as a significant upgrade to the existing Quickplace product line. This product has been maturing over many years, and this new release provides many new capabilities. These include native support for wikis and blogs "out of the box".

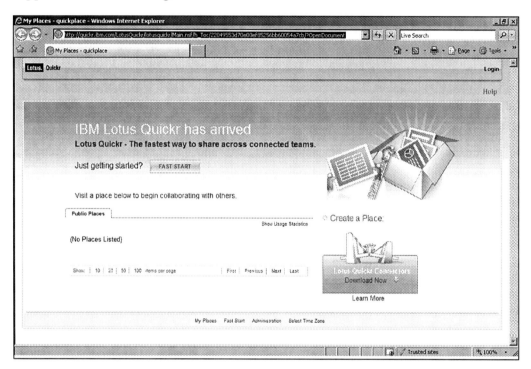

Product Installation

The basic installation process for Quickr with service for Domino is very simple. It involves installing a base Domino server v7.0.2 FP1. The Quickr product components are then installed on top of this server.

Directory Integration

After installation, there is some additional configuration required depending on the intended usage.

- **User/group directory configuration** is used to control the authorization and authentication of the environment.

- **Sametime integration** is used to enable presence awareness within the places.
- **QPServlet configuration** is used for WebSphere Portal integration.

The user/group directory configuration allows you to select one of three directory types:

- **Internal place level directory** allows for registration of users at a place level. The users are independent of any corporate directory that may be in place. Generally this is used to support external user access.

- **Lotus Domino directory** allows users and groups to be stored in the `names.nsf` database (public address book) and corresponding directories surfaced via directory assistance.

- **LDAP directory** allows for users in a supported native LDAP directory (for example, Domino, IBM Tivoli Directory Server, Microsoft Active Directory, Novelle Directory, or Sun One Directory). This configuration allows for the refinement of the settings used to interact with the LDAP source.

The directory can be configured by first logging as an administrative user. In the screen below, we have logged in as user **Admin** from the Domino directory.

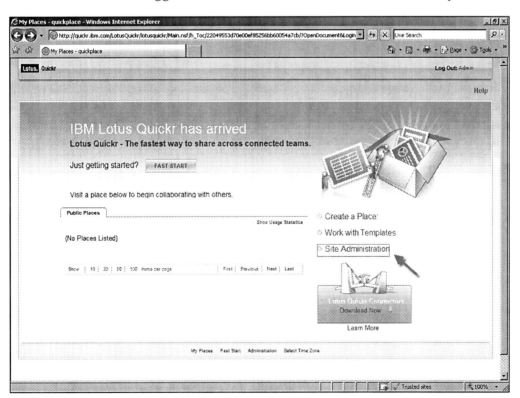

Next, select the **User Directory** option from **Site Administration**. The following screen shows the default value of **No Directory** selected. This is the base setup where the `contacts.nsf` database for each place will be used as a user directory.

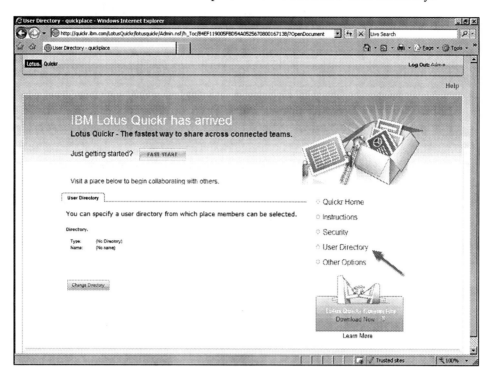

It is possible to change the user directory by clicking the **Change Directory** button. This lets you choose between **No Directory**, **LDAP Server**, and **Domino Server**.

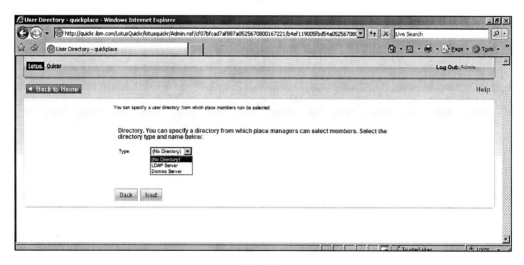

If LDAP Server is selected, then options for connecting to the directory server will be displayed as shown in the screen below:

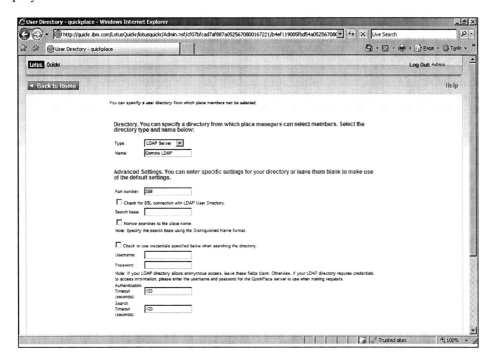

This screen contains the following fields:

- **Name** provides the host name of the LDAP Directory Server.
- **Port number** is the LDAP TCP/IP port used to communicate with the server.
- **Check for SSL connection with LDAP User Directory** enables SSL encryption of the LDAP traffic. Note that this is an "all or nothing" selection. It is not possible to only encrypt parts of the conversation with the LDAP server.
- **Search base** controls determines where in the LDAP tree to search for users and groups. For a Domino LDAP directory this value is generally left blank. This is because groups in Domino as seen through LDAP have no organizational component (for example, cn=Sales Users).
- **Narrow searches to the place name** further restrict the LDAP search to users that contain the Quickr place name (for instance, Sales).
- **Check to use credentials specified below when searching the directory** controls whether or not anonymous access is used for the LDAP directory. It is very common to have read-only binding credentials to search the directory.

- **Username** provides the user's distinguished Name for the LDAP server (for example, `cn=quickrbind,ou=Admin,o=Acme`).

- **Password** is the password for the user name above.

- **Authentication timeout** controls the time in seconds for the login operation to timeout. The default is 120 seconds.

- **Search timeout** controls the time in seconds for LDAP searches to timeout. The default is 120 seconds.

The next section of the directory configuration screen determines whether or not new users can be controlled at the place level. Specifically this allows for the place manager to create new users that are not in the directory. Otherwise they can only add users that exist in the directory.

New Users. Do you want to allow place managers to create new users in each place, or require managers to select existing users only from the available directory?

⊙ Allow managers to create new users in each place.

○ Disallow new users - Require managers to select *existing* users from the available directory.

After you complete the configuration, the LDAP directory is available for use. If additional configuration is needed beyond this, then a `qpconfig.xml` file must be used. This file is created in the Quickr server data directory, where there is a sample configuration file called `qpconfig_sample.xml`.

The `qpconfig.xml` file can be used to fine tune the LDAP directory settings including attribute mappings, LDAP search filters.

If Lotus Domino is selected as the directory type, the only option is management of the place level security. This is the same option as in the LDAP server setting.

Lotus Sametime Integration

The process required to configure Sametime integration with Quickr is similar. From the **Site Administration** screen, select **Other Options** and then select **Edit Options**.

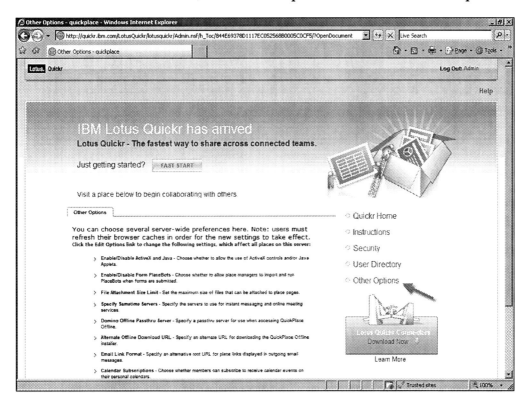

The **Sametime Servers** section controls the host names to be used for the Quickr server. This screen has numerous other items as well that are covered in the administration help.

Sametime Servers. To enable real-time collaboration features in QuickPlace, you need to specify the Community Server that will provide awareness and instant messaging services, and the Meeting Server that will provide meeting services. The same Sametime server can be used for both functions if required. Leave blank if you want to disable the features.

| Sametime Community Server: | st.ibm.com | [protocol://]hostname[:port], Example: http://myserver.mycompany.com |
| Sametime Meeting Server: | st.ibm.com | [protocol://]hostname[:port], Example: http://myserver.mycompany.com |

Enter the Sametime Community and meeting server host names. Depending on the environment, these may be the same hosts.

Quickr depends on SSO to be correctly configured between the Quickr and Sametime servers. This allows for the user credentials from the Quickr server to be passed into Sametime. By default the Quickr server will only have basic authentication configured.

The next configuration step is to set up a new Web SSO document in to Domino directory shared by the Quickr and Sametime servers. (If you are using WebSphere Portal server as shown in a later section, this Web SSO document will contain the imported WebSphere application server token.)

You must now copy several files from the Sametime server to the Quickr server. These files will be used for both awareness and meeting services. The final step is to ensure that the **Chat: Shot the Chat** link is enabled. It should be enabled by default.

Integration with Lotus Sametime and Quickr services for Domino involves the qpconfig.xml file. It manages the Sametime features available within Quickr. When using Sametime with Quickr, only users that are in the LDAP directory will be visible. Any locally created users will not have awareness.

Application Development

The final integration component of Quickr with services for WebSphere Portal and Domino comes in the area of application development. Since this edition of Quickr is built on top of a Domino foundation, it is possible to use traditional Domino development techniques to customize and extend it in many ways.

Quickr with Services for WebSphere Portal

The WebSphere Portal based edition of Quickr represents a significant application in the Web 2.0 space. It heavily leverages these technologies to bring an industry leading collaboration experience. This product expands on the capabilities originally created from IBM Workplace Collaboration Services and IBM Workplace Services Express.

The user interface is very similar to the Domino based edition. The feature sets between these two are different at the moment. Therefore it is important for customers to evaluate the requirements for each place to determine if the Domino or J2EE foundation provides the necessary features.

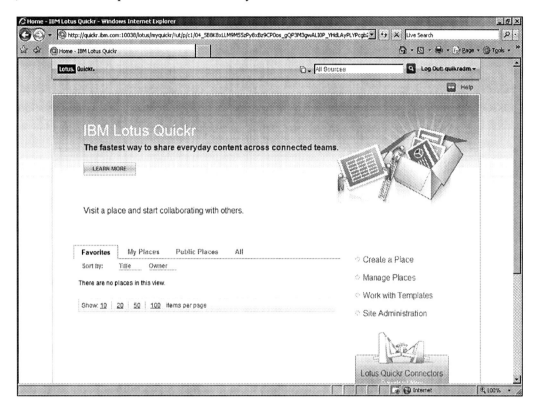

Product Installation

The installation of Quickr services for WebSphere Portal server has been optimized for ease of deployment.

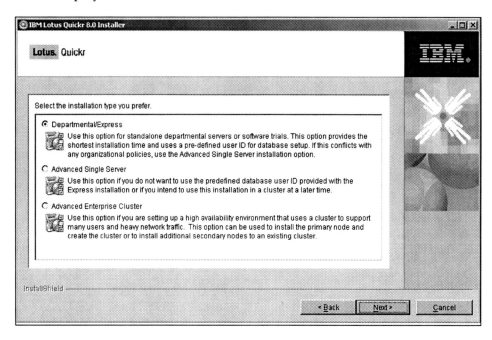

There are three installation types that are available in the setup program.

- **Departmental/Express** provides for the fastest deployment. The server is fully deployed with all necessary components including DB2.

- **Advanced Single Server** allows for additional options during setup for future expansion.

- **Advanced Enterprise Cluster** allows for a base installation that is intended for a clustered deployment.

Additional details about the product installation are available in the Quickr administration guide.

Directory Integration

Since the J2EE based version of Quickr is built on top of the WebSphere application server and the WebSphere Portal server, there are only two directory configurations:

- **Custom User Registry** is the internal directory built in on top of the Quickr RDBMS.
- **LDAP User Registry** is the external LDAP directory.

Even though you have to transfer security to an external LDAP directory as a separate step, it should not be inferred that security is not enabled in Quickr. The installation process enables WebSphere Portal security against the custom user registry with a user specified during the installation. This user is `quikradm` by default.

The custom user registry is similar to the default Domino edition of Quickr. That is, the place administrators can manage new users without having them written into the corporate directory. When using an LDAP user registry, it is common for these to have write access restricted limiting the creation of new users outside of the Directory administration team. The process of security transfer to an external LDAP source is handled by the Configuration Wizard.

It is recommended that, if you are planning to transfer security to an external LDAP directory, this should be done during the initial installation. It is technically possible to do this transfer with data in the system, but you risk causing harm to that information later. This is particularly true if your user credentials are changing as part of this move.

In preparation for the security transfer, several users and groups need to be created in the LDAP directory.

- **wpsadmin**: WebSphere Portal server administrative user account.
- **wpsbind**:LDAP bind user account.
- **wasadmin**: WebSphere application aerver administrative user account.
- **wpsadmins**: WebSphere Portal server administrative group account; this should contain wpsadmin user account at a minimum.
- **wpsContentAdministators**: WebSphere web content manager administrative group. This should contain the same users as wpsadmins as a minimum.
- **wpsDocReviewer**: WebSphere Portal document manager administrative group. This should contain the same users as wpsadmins as a minimum.

It is possible to use different names for these entries as needed.

The specific process for the security transfer is beyond the scope of this chapter. It is very similar to that used for WebSphere Portal itself. Refer to the Quickr administration guide for additional information.

Sametime Integration

The use of awareness within Quickr services for WebSphere Portal is configured in the same as any other WebSphere Portal installation:

1. Configure the Sametime server using the LDAP directory. It is possible to use the native Domino directory for Sametime, but integration is easier if WebSphere Portal/Quickr and Sametime are both using LDAP.

2. Configure SSO between WebSphere Portal/Quickr and Sametime. This is accomplished by exporting the LTPA token value from the WebSphere application server and importing it into the Domino domain hosting the Sametime servers.

3. Update the `wpconfig.properties` file for WebSphere Portal/Quickr with the values for the Sametime server. This includes the following:
   Sametime host name
   Sametime protocol (http)
   Sametime http port

4. There are additional configuration options available in the `CSEnvironment.properties` file to facilitate name mapping, if a different directory is used for Sametime.

5. Run the `WPSconfig.bat/.sh lcc-configure-sametime` configuration program to name the necessary system changes.

Lotus Quickr Connectors

One of the key features of Quickr is the openness provided by the connector architecture. These connectors allow for direct interaction with the Quickr servers independently of the backend architecture (WebSphere Portal/Domino).

The installation of these is via the large link on the main page of either edition.

The preceding link will initiate the download and installation of the connectors package. This is handled as a standard `msi` package starting you at the welcome screen. Click **Next** to continue.

Next is the license text. After you have read all of the content and gotten agreement from your legal department, click **Next** to continue. The next screen allows for a custom setup of the Connectors. Select the desired options and click **Next**.

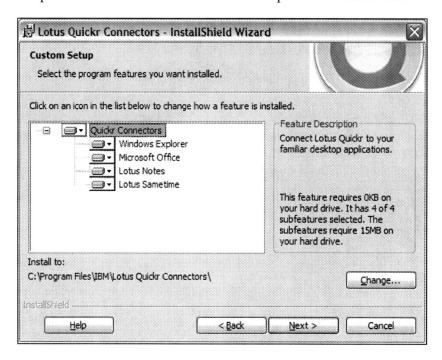

If you select Notes as a Quickr Connector type, you will be asked for the file page of the Notes client installation. Change the path if necessary to match your installation and click **Next**.

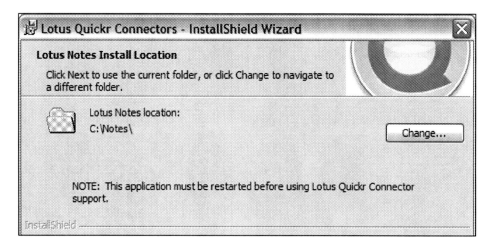

If you select Sametime as a Quickr Connector type, you will be asked for the file page of the Sametime client installation. Change the path if necessary to match your installation and click **Next**.

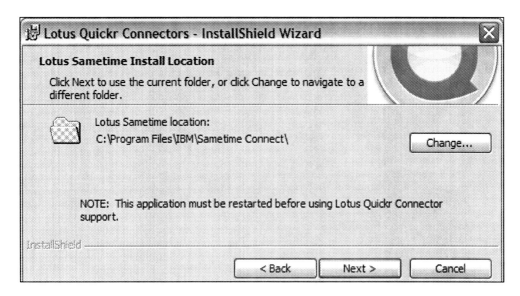

The connector will now be installed on your machine.

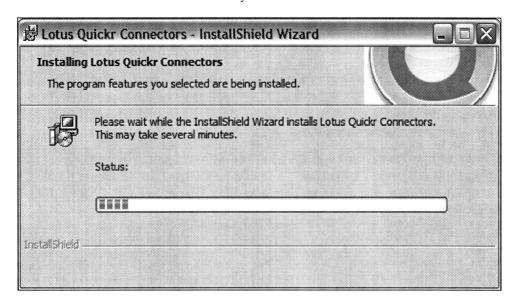

After the installation process has completed, the following screen will appear. The two options can remain selected if necessary. It is advised to at least launch the Microsoft Windows Explorer connector. This will allow you to add Quickr servers to the configuration.

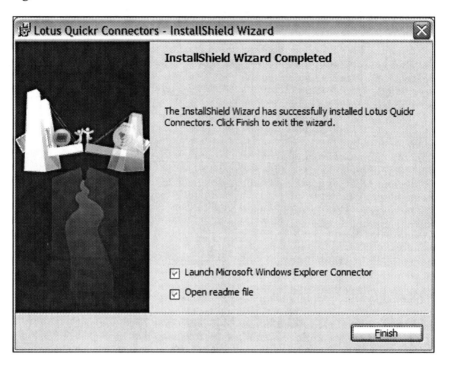

From the Quickr icon on the Microsoft Windows task bar, select **Add Places** to install your first connection to a Quickr server. At least one connection is necessary. It does not matter if this is pointing to a J2EE or Domino edition backend, as both will function the same via the connectors.

In the **Add Places** section of **Lotus Quickr Connectors** dialog, enter the server path and user credentials for server. This could be different for different Quickr servers, depending on the directory configuration. After entering the information, select **Next**.

If the connection to the server was successful, the following dialog should appear. This will be a list of places that are present on the server for you to interface with. Select the desired place from the list. It is possible to select multiple places. Then select **Finish**.

The monitor is a background process that communicates with the various Quickr instances and places. To access the monitor, select the Quickr icon from the task bar.

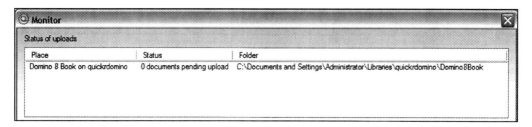

Now that the Quickr Connector is configured, it will be visible in the various applications. Below is an example of the Microsoft Windows Explorer connector. It allows Quickr to work like a file server to drag and drop files. This also has the document management features of check in, check out, and versions.

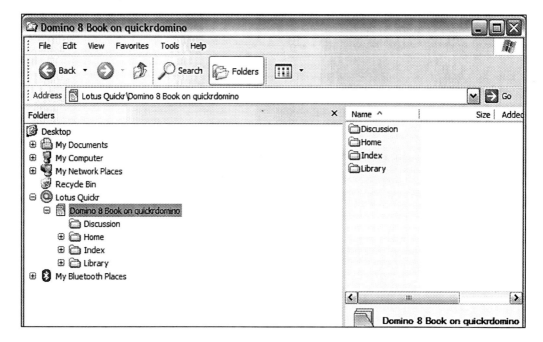

Within Notes, Quickr connectors are visible from the **Actions** menu. This allows interaction with the Quickr services to provide links to content and save file attachments into the content store.

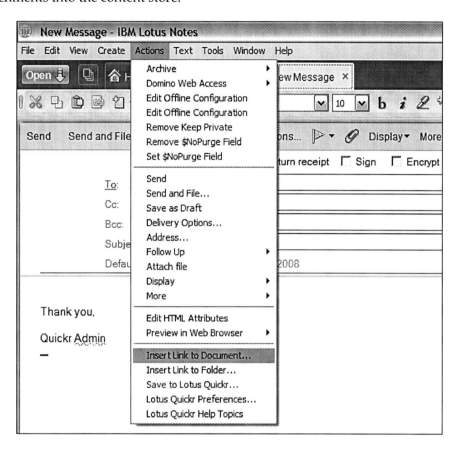

The following screen is called **Insert Link to Document**. It allows a user to send a link to a document in the Quickr content store instead of putting it in an email message. This allows different users to access a central copy of the content. In the **Add Link** dialog, you can select a document from the navigator. Select **Open** to add the link to the mail message or other Notes document.

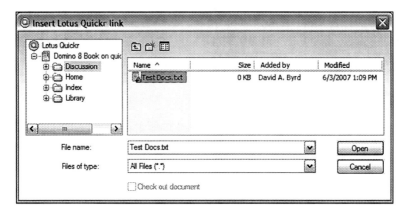

After the link has been added to the email message, others can use it to open the content.

The connector for Sametime allows access to Quickr content stores. It is implemented as a Lotus Expeditor plug-in within the Sametime 7.5.1 client.

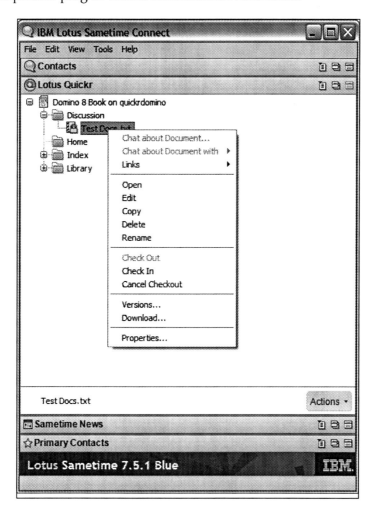

The connector for Microsoft Office provides access to Quickr document management functions directly from within Office applications.

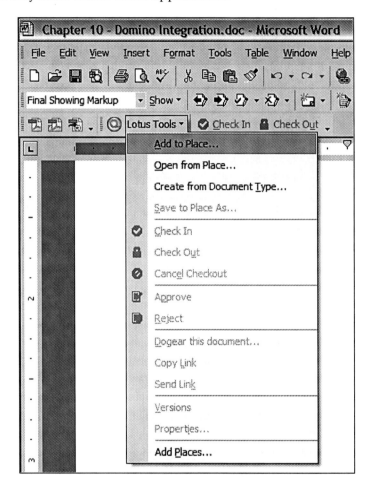

As you can see, the Lotus Quickr connectors provide for tight integration into the content. This will give the end users choices as to how they work and interact with their content.

Lotus Sametime

Sametime is an enterprise client instant messaging and web conferencing product that has been available for many years. The current version of 7.5.1 extends these capabilities with a revised web conference meeting center client and Lotus Expeditor based instant messaging client.

The product is a core component of the unified communications and collaboration strategy. This represents an integrated messaging solution that includes instant messaging, voice, and video.

The client product now supports not only Windows, but also Linux and Mac OS X. These additional client platform choices expand its enterprise reach.

The 7.5.1 product release introduces a new server platform with Linux. This has been a long sought after operating system for the server platform.

Product Installation

The installation of Sametime 7.5.1 requires Domino 7.0.1 or higher. The Domino server is used for the HTTP services, configuration, and meeting data storage. A slight variation on this is the Enterprise Meeting Server (EMS) product. It extends the capabilities of Sametime with the WebSphere application server as the front end. The main difference is that EMS provides meeting services fail-over. While the WebSphere application server is used as the front end, the engine driving the meetings themselves is a standard Sametime server running on Domino.

The installation process involves running the Sametime server installation wizard on an existing server. After you answer a few simple questions, the installation will complete in a matter of a few minutes. After this base installation has been completed, additional customization is possible.

One important thing to note is that Sametime Connect clients are not installed as part of the Sametime server. The installation programs for these must be installed after the base server install.

There is a Sametime SDK toolkit that can be installed as part of the base package. This provides API services and sample applications to build integrated solutions.

Directory Integration

The base installation itself is fairly simple with a minimal amount of questions. The key difference is the directory type selection of either Domino or LDAP. Regardless of user directory type, the base functions of Sametime are the same.

If the Domino directory is used, then the configuration is very straightforward. The Sametime server needs a replica copy of the Domain directory. It also needs a Web SSO document defined so as to function correctly. This is done by default as part of the Sametime setup if such a document does not already exist.

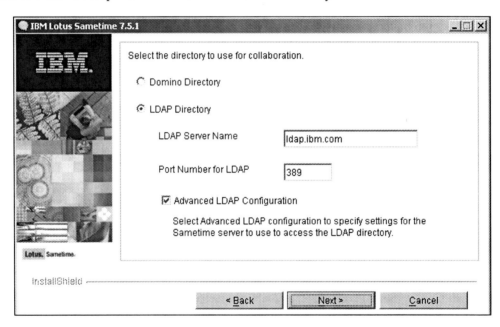

If an LDAP directory is used, then the configuration can be a bit more complicated. During the installation process, you will be asked for the LDAP server host name and port number. Further configuration is handled via the Sametime administration Web interface or by editing the `stconfig.nsf` database via a Notes client.

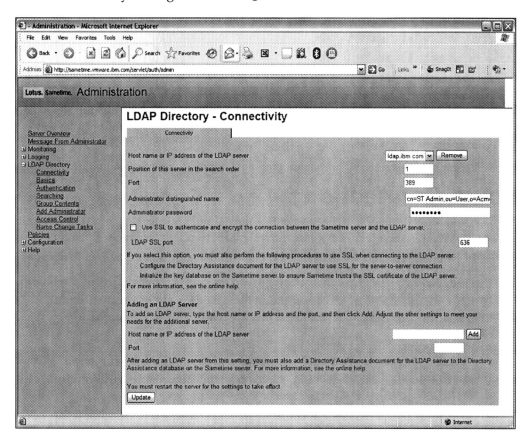

When an LDAP directory is used in Domino, it has two interface points. The first is for instant messaging. These services directly access the LDAP server and don't use Domino. The second is for meeting services. These use the Domino's directory's assistance database to interact with the LDAP source. The reason behind this is that meeting services leverages the Domino authentication services and database ACLs to manage access.

Application Integration

Sametime has many integration points. This is in addition to the Lotus Expeditor based client.

- Notes Sideshelf.
- Notes view/document integration (for instance, inbox).
- Quickplace/Quickr.
- The WebSphere Portal server.

This list includes a few integration points that are available. The key is that the Sametime services can be integrated into virtually any application that can leverage the API services it provides.

Lotus Connections

The Lotus Connections product represents a new classification of applications within the enterprise. It is targeted as a social network tool to allow for dynamic end user collaboration through Web 2.0 tools and technologies.

The product has five key areas that it brings into an environment. Each of these can be deployed separately or mixed and matched as needed. However, to fully take advantage of this product, all five should work in unison. The five areas are as follows:

- **Profiles** provide for personal information about end users within the environment. This can include reporting structures, contact information, and associated content within the remaining four components.
- **Communities** provide for a collaboration environment based upon the wiki structure.
- **Blogs** provide for basic blogging services for an enterprise.
- **Dogear** provides for intelligent bookmarking services across all of the Lotus Connections application. It also has the ability to bookmark any linkable material such as a website, Notes documents, Quickr content. One key aspect is the nature of social bookmarking, where an individual can subscribe to the bookmarks of other interested parties.
- **Activities** provide for a new task based work management tool. An activity is a discrete work stream that can consist of one or more components and can involve many individuals. An example activity would be the creation of a book such as this. The book itself would be the activity with many active participants. Then as content is created, reviewed, and updated, those activities can be managed in the context of the activity.

Each of these components with the exception of profiles provides the ability to enter unique tags. The tags themselves then roll up as tag clouds.

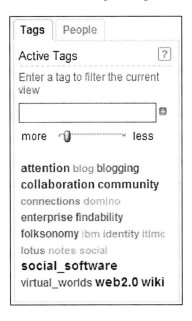

These tag clouds allow for quick information categorization and searching. Each tag cloud also provides for a slider to increase or decrease the depth of information displayed. If you have not seen these before, the font size and color indicates the strength of the tag or its frequency of occurrence.

Within Notes/Domino, the main point of contact is in the area of activities and Dogear. These two items can directly connect into the Notes 8 client.

Activities are rendered as a side shelf within the client. It is available as a right-click context menu that can be used t add a Notes document (such as an email) to an activity.

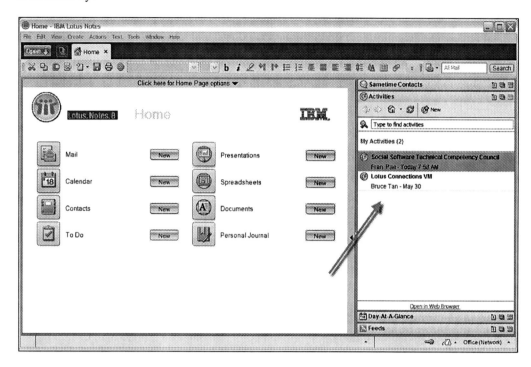

Dogear is available as a right click context menu.

The architecture and installation for Lotus Connections is based on WebSphere application server. For additional information, see the Lotus Connections administration guide.

Summary

In this chapter, we looked as several add-on products that are typical integrated into a Notes/Domino environment. These include Quickplace/Quickr, Sametime, and Lotus Connections. Each of these represents is a key component for the software environment at your company.

As we mentioned, there are a number of other Lotus/IBM products that can be integrated into Notes/Domino. For more information, consult http://www.lotus.com.

Third-Party Products

In this appendix, we look at several vendor offerings that could extend your Lotus Notes/Domino 8 environment. The information contained in this chapter is provided by the vendors themselves. For more information, consult the respective vendor's website.

PistolStar

PistolStar, Inc. is a password management software solutions provider specializing in IBM software platforms, with a core focus on the Lotus software suite. Many of PistolStar's senior-level developers are from Iris and Lotus, bringing in-depth knowledge and first hand experience to Password Power 8's plug-ins.

PistolStar's Password Power 8 plug-ins expand the authentication and password management capabilities of Lotus Notes/Domino 8. The Notes ID plug-in offers SSO and seamless redirection of the Notes ID file's authentication to LDAP compliant directories (e.g. Microsoft Active Directory, Novell eDirectory, Tivoli Directory Server). Likewise, the Domino plug-in offers HTTP SSO to Domino and seamless redirection of HTTP authentication to LDAP-compliant directories as well. The **Web Set Password Plug-in (WSP)** offers great control over the management of the Domino Internet password if it is vital to the current authentication processes. Below is an outline of the functionality available with each of PistolStar's Password Power 8 plug-ins as they pertain to Lotus Notes and Domino 8.

To achieve PistolStar's definition of **Single Sign-On (SSO)**, we start at the desktop with the Windows session. We leverage Microsoft Active Directory and Novell eDirectory—both significant technologies in Windows-centric computer environments—by enabling use of either of their passwords at the initial computer login to access all Domino server applications in multiple domains and the Notes client. With this capability, the number of times an end-user must supply logon information during a Windows session is reduced to a single instance.

Password Power 8 Domino Plug-in

The Domino plug-in provides end-users with SSO access to all applications on Domino servers, creating convenience and saving login time. The Domino plug-in now offers two methods for SSO capabilities: Kerberos or proprietary cookies, both of which optionally allow authentication utilizing a Personless NAB.

Enabling SSO to Domino HTTP servers via Kerberos requires connectivity to a central Key Distribution Center (KDC). In Windows, each Active Directory domain controller acts as a KDC. Users authenticate themselves to services (e.g. Domino servers) by first authenticating to their Windows machine using a domain account, then requesting encrypted service tickets from the KDC for the specific services they wish to use. This last step is performed automatically by the user's web browser. Only the service (and the KDC) can decrypt the service ticket to get the user's information. Because only the KDC could have created the service ticket, the service knows that the user must have also authenticated to the KDC so it can trust the user credentials in that ticket.

Alternatively, to enable SSO to Domino HTTP servers, a web browser toolbar creates client-side cookies with encrypted credentials for each of the Domino servers listed in the Password Power configuration file. Accessing a Domino server through a web browser automatically sends the corresponding cookie with the request. These same cookies can also be used to grant SSO to IBM Lotus QuickPlace and Sametime, IBM WebSphere and WebSphere Portal and SAP Netweaver. These in-memory session cookies have a configurable expiration interval that defaults to 12 hours. When the end-user closes the browser, logs out or shuts down Windows, the cookies are automatically destroyed.

The Domino plug-in also supports a Personless NAB allowing the end-user to logon to Domino HTTP with their network directory (e.g. Microsoft Active Directory) credentials to access all Domino HTTP solutions, including Lotus iNotes, Sametime, QuickPlace, and Domino Web applications. Browser-only end-users no longer need a duplicate set of Person documents as the Domino plug-in requires that the end-user be defined only once – in Active Directory (users of the stand-alone Notes client would still need Person documents to support encryption and signatures). The Personless NAB approach also leverages Domino's Directory Assistance, which allows an end-user access token to contain their Active Directory name and any Active Directory groups to which they belong. The central role in this approach is performed by a DSAPI filter which can give SSO and overrides the normal authentication process, which checks the username and password against the Domino Directory.

This functionality solves many of the username mapping issues associated with authenticating against remote directories without requiring changes to the LDAP server accounts or Domino Directory. Redirecting web authentication requests from the Domino Directory to a different LDAP directory also eliminates the need to maintain or synchronize the Domino Internet password, as its presence and upkeep are no longer required. This functionality extends to affect all Domino HTTP authentication including QuickPlace and Sametime.

System Requirements for Domino Plug-in (Server-Side)

- Lotus Domino 5/6/7/8
- Microsoft Windows NT, 2000, 2003
- IBM AIX 5.1 and higher
- IBM System i V5R3 and higher
- All x86 Linux distributions
- Sun Solaris SPARC 9 and higher
- LDAP Server – Microsoft Active Directory, Novell eDirectory, SunONE/iPlanet, Domino, Tivoli Directory Server
- SAP Netweaver 2004 (optional)
- WebSphere 5.1+ (optional)
- WebSphere Portal 5.1+ (optional)

Password Power 8 Notes ID Plug-in

PistolStar's Password Power Notes ID plug-in removes the need for separate passwords and repositories for the Notes ID file by configuring the Active Directory as the central password authentication point for accessing the Lotus Notes Client, thus eliminating the need to separately maintain the Notes ID password.

The Notes ID plug-in provides synchronization between Active Directory and the Notes ID File and allows forgotten Notes ID file passwords to be automatically recovered and resynchronized with the Active Directory.

With PistolStar's Password Power Notes Id plug-in, a successful authentication to Microsoft Active Directory, Novell eDirectory, Lotus Domino LDAP, Tivoli Directory Server or Sun ONE LDAP grants access to the Lotus Notes client. This effectively eliminates the manual Notes ID password recovery by allowing a reset of the LDAP password to restore access to Lotus Notes. Password synchronization between LDAP and the Notes ID file is always performed for times when the LDAP server is unreachable.

System Requirements for Notes ID Plug-in (Client Side)

- Windows 2000 Professional, XP Professional or Vista
- Lotus Notes client 5/6/7/8 for Windows (optional)

(No browser is required for the Notes ID plug-in)

Password Power 8 Web Set Password Plug-in

This plug-in synchronizes multiple passwords via a web browser. This allows end-users to synchronize Windows, HTTP, LDAP passwords and Notes ID File. This increases security because having only one password to commit to memory decreases the likelihood end-users will write it down and become a target for internal intruders.

System Requirement for Web Set Password Plug-in

- Lotus Domino 5/6/7/8
- Microsoft Windows NT, 2000, 2003
- IBM AIX 5.1 and higher
- IBM System i V5R3 and higher
- All x86 Linux distributions
- Sun Solaris SPARC 8 and higher
- Lotus Sametime 3.1, 6.5.1, 7, 7.5 *(optional)*
- Lotus QuickPlace 3.1, 6.5.1, 7 *(optional)*
- Domino.doc 6.5.1, 7 *(optional)*

Security

The Password Power 8 Web Set Password plug-in (WSP) offers the following security features:

- **Force an SSL connection for logins**: WSP can ensure end-users' credentials are submitted via SSL. If an end-user tries to login through HTTP instead of HTTPS, WSP forces login with HTTPS by redirecting the end-user to a HTTPS connection.
- **Dictionary lookup functionality**: Allows administrators to enable a dictionary lookup to prevent users from setting pre-specified (unacceptable or easily guessed) passwords, such as company name. The lookup can be added in three ways: Notes database, JavaScript, or both Notes database and a list accessed through JavaScript.

- **Password quality**: With WSP, Administrators can configure several fully customizable password 'strength' rules.

- **Password quality check on both client and server sides**: With WSP, client side checking does not access server and is done through JavaScript requiring less server loan and network traffic. Server side checking can use @PasswordQuality instead of JavaScript (requires a trip to the server) to determine if a new password is acceptable. This allows administrators to set minimum password quality (0-16) and any new password must, at a minimum, equal this quality.

- **Disqualify username as password**: Administrators can prevent new passwords from containing variations of the end-user's username, a typical password choice that is easily guessed by network intruders.

- **Password expiration grace period**: WSP lets Administrators select a grace period or a timeframe in which end-users must change their passwords.

- **Disable Internet Explorer Auto Complete**: Administrators can prevent Internet Explorer Auto Complete feature from offering a list of previously used entries. When enabled, this applies to all WSP fields and only affects IS5.0 and higher. This feature prevents internal intruders from easily accessing the password from the drop-down menu of previously used passwords.

- **Prevent similar password use**: WSP's 'Prevent Similar Passwords' JavaScript Rule checking disallows use of similar passwords during password resets.

- **Confirmation requirement for self-registration**: With WSP, an email is sent to the end-user with a link to a confirmation page for self-registration. On this page, end-users are prompted for their email address, which affects creation of the Person Document in the Domino Directory.

Auditing Features

WSP also includes auditing features. These include:

- **Store last login date and time**: Allows Administrators to track the date and time an end-user last logged in – data that is stored as a new field in the Person Document. Administrators can also elect to record more detailed information to be sent to the WSP database, such as username, end-user's IP address, URL requested and server name.

- **Enable Strikeout logging functionality**: Strikeouts can be logged to a database so Administrators see when failed attempts occurred.

- **Log invalid usernames**: Administrators can enable logging of invalid usernames to the mail-in database. The information included in this report is:
  - IP address of computer that made the request
  - URL requested by the user
  - Username used
  - Password given
  - The WSP-specific function the user attempted to accomplish (log in, set password, and so on)
  - The server on which the attempt occurred
  - The time the attempt occurred

- **Enable 'set password' logging**: In WSP, Administrators can enable logging of successful 'Set Password' events to the mail-in database.

Help Desk

WSP also includes Help Desk productivity features. For example, WSP's Help Desk Manager Utility allows Help Desk personnel to manage end-user passwords without full access to WSP's configuration data. This database includes several actions (the Unlock Agent item is actually an agent, not a button):

- **Unlock User** unlocks end-user accounts that have been locked by WSP's strikeout function utility.

- **Email Random Password**: generates random value passwords and emails them to the end-user. This can also be used automatically send multiple end-user's blank passwords.

- **Reset Password** resets the HTTP password to a new value when an end-user does not have an HTTP password, has forgotten it, is unable to reset it themselves, and does not have a Notes client.

- **Expire Password** forces end-user to change their HTTP password the next time they log in to Domino through a Web browser. This is useful when password policies change.

- **Reset WSP Fields** resets end-user accounts as if they had never accessed WSP.

- **Set Expiration Date** provides a one-time override of WSP's expiration functionality. This is useful for exempting end-users from resetting a password.

- **Unlock Agent** unlocks end-users automatically every x number of hours.

In addition, WSP offers the following features designed to assist Help Desk personnel:

- **Enable customized HTML**: With WSP, Administrators can write customized messages to end-users to prompt them through the login process, reducing end-user confusion and subsequent Help Desk Calls.

- **Email Random Password Functionality**: Allows Administrators to generate random passwords that are automatically emailed to new end-users. This is both an administrative time-saver as well as a security feature because the administrator never sees the password. WSP enables customizable expiration options for the new password as well.

- **Support localization**: Administrators can configure **all** UI screens in any language **without** use/knowledge of Domino Designer. Administrators can easily modify logon screens to ensure that customized messages and prompts are understood by the end-user. Localization reduces Help Desk calls by minimizing end-user confusion.

- **Enable customized disclaimer messages**: Administrators can create a disclaimer message that the end-user sees upon logon. This feature can be used to display corporate network usage instructions for sensitive Websites and resources (i.e., password protected).

- **Easily configurable user interface**: All WSP screens seen by the end-user are configurable **without** knowledge/use of Domino Designer. Through a user-friendly interface, screens can be modified with logo insertion, font and color selection, and editing of HTML seen by user.

- **WSP Unlock Utility**: WSP's strikeout functionality is an important part of securing the authentication process. When enabled, the end-user is no longer able to log in after a pre-set number of attempts. The WSP Unlock Utility allows Help Desk personnel who do not have Editor-level access to the Domino directories to unlock end-users who have struck out.

You can now delegate unlocking of strikeouts to Help Desk personnel with less security clearance. This is especially beneficial to companies with employees in different time zones, when employing Help Desk personnel with a high-level of security clearance around the clock is costly. The end-user does not have to wait for support and the company can maintain security by granting Editor-level access to fewer personnel.

End Users

WSP also offers end-user productivity features. For instance, WSP's challenge, question, and answer functionality allows the end-user to recover passwords without Help Desk assistance. This feature stems potential security breaches that occur when Administrators e-mail passwords to end-users or when they give out passwords to end-users over the phone. Challenge questions are customizable.

WSP also allows end-users to create their own user accounts without administrator involvement. If more complex workflow around account verification is necessary, self-registrations can be set to require either end-user confirmation (to prevent automated account creation bots) or approval by an internal user.

Finally

For more information about PistolStar and Password Power 8 plug-ins please visit our website www.pistolstar.com. Or you may contact:

PistolStar, Inc.
PO Box 1226
Amherst, NH 03031 US
(603) 546-2300

Reporting from Lotus Notes and Domino Data

As a Notes/ Domino developer, you must be familiar with the limitations of reporting from Notes and Domino data. Common approaches include using Notes scripting or external reporting tools to transform the data into meaningful reports that can be accessed on demand by end users.

This section provides a quick overview of the two methods, their inherent limitations and provides an introduction to IntelliPRINT, the only effective reporting solution which is native to Notes and Domino. The section on IntelliPRINT lists a few of its key features which make it an effective solution for addressing the need for reporting from Notes and Domino data, in a holistic manner.

There are two common approaches generally followed by organizations to report and print data from Notes and Domino.

Reporting Based on Notes Programming using Lotus Script

Notes professionals often prefer to create and manage their reports programmatically using Lotus Script. This approach ensures that data security and integrity are preserved, the business context is inherited, and the Notes application workflow is kept intact. While it overcomes many limitations set by non-native reporting tools, reporting using Lotus Script does have a few limitations:

- **Time Consuming**: The time taken to create reports may vary from several hours for basic reports to several days for complex reports.

- **Significant overhead on IT**: Programming requires highly competent Notes developers to design and manage the reports. This imposes time and effort overheads on the IT team.

- **Limited Reporting Functionality**: Visual representation of data in the form of charts is not supported, and even tabular reports often require the creation of additional views.

This approach is time consuming, expensive and end-user unfriendly. In most situations, user request for reports cannot be met due to the effort involved in producing the report and the poor presentation quality of the reports.

Reporting Based on Tools External to Notes

There are a wide variety of report creation tools with extensive functionality that are available for use with Notes and Domino. However, most of these are not native to the Notes and Domino framework. These tools connect to Notes data by using ODBC drivers or by exporting Notes data to other formats such as spreadsheets. Limitations posed by these approaches include:

- **Security**: Once data leaves the Notes environment via ODBC, it compromises the robust data security offered by Notes and fails to leverage the Notes ACL which is one of the inherent strengths of Lotus technology. Data integrity is also compromised, as data type definitions are lost when the data is exported from Notes. Furthermore, the exported data can be modified, as most external environments do not provide the robust change tracking inherent to Notes. This compromises the reliability and accuracy of reported data.

- **Performance**: There is a significant performance impact while accessing or exporting data from Notes and Domino through the ODBC connector. The performance degradation results in significant additional hardware investment and compromises business efficiency by considerably increasing system response times.

- **Inability to use native Notes functionalities**: Unique Notes functionalities such as @Formula, multi-value fields, RTF, etc. cannot be used for designing reports

- **Presents a confusing view of the target database**: Notes forms, views and folders are exposed as separate data tables leading to a confused view of the target database

Introducing IntelliPRINT Reporting

IntelliPRINT started as a printing solution for Notes and Domino and has matured to become one of the best reporting solutions in its current release, which was launched at Lotusphere 2007. It has also been extended to natively support Notes/ Domino 8 while continuing support for Notes versions 6 and 7.

IntelliPRINT Reporting is to Notes and Domino what Crystal Reports was to Visual Basic. It is a native reporting component that is tightly integrated with the Notes and Domino application framework. It is a logical extension to Notes and Domino and lets you use its APIs to tightly integrate the reports within the workflow of your Notes and Domino applications.

As the report format is stored as a Notes document, security settings for report access as well as row level access are automatically inherited from the Notes ACL. The report is then presented as a Notes tab making the reporting workflow integral to your application workflow.

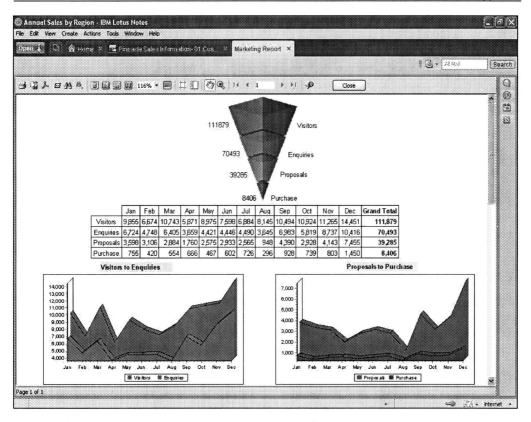

The key features that make it a logical extension of Notes and Domino are listed below and include details of the steps involved in creating a simple report and a complex report.

Report Deployment without Development Overheads

Consider a scenario where a multi-level cross-tab report has to be created, such as a sales report that shows the sales for multiple products across several geographical regions. The rows would display the sales for each of the regions while the columns would show the product sales across the regions. Creating such a cross-tab by just using Lotus Script would typically entail the following:

- Several hours of scripting to create the row and column totals

- A script that spans several hundred lines

- Creation of additional views in the Notes application, for document selection in the script

- Hard coding of the font and color formatting

The same cross-tab can be created with IntelliPRINT Reporting within just a few minutes. The benefits of using IntelliPRINT in this situation include:

- Drag and drop creation process that saves substantial time
- No changes required in the database
- The Notes database would not get loaded with multiple Views
- Color schemes can be easily and quickly defined to suit organizational standards
- Presentation quality reports that can be printed or exported to PDF

IntelliPRINT thus helps reduce a substantial amount of IT workload for not only creation of the report but also for future changes in the report! The report format gets saved in the host database and can be accessed on demand by authorized users.

Report Deployment without Administrative Overhead

Once designed, a report template is stored in the host Notes application or a central report repository. These formats can also be deployed on a Domino server and made available online via a web browser. Report format take very little space to store — typically less than 100KB — and can be opened almost instantaneously.

When a report is viewed, data is fetched from the database and presented in the format as specified in the report metadata. This ensures the report always reflects real-time information. Generated reports can be programmatically stored, for example you could save them into the same Notes database as the application.

IntelliPRINT Reporting integrates seamlessly with the Notes and Domino's existing security framework. Reports are only accessible to users who have access to the applications in which IntelliPRINT is embedded. In addition, report creators can specify access controls for individual reports in addition to the Notes ACLs already present. This means the data in IntelliPRINT reports have access controls enabled for users as well as groups. Report Designers can easily set this up using a form, which will specify access levels for each report. This ensures that your users can access their data within Notes' secure, consistent security model without you having to spend time and effort to setup different systems.

Integration with The Application Workflow

Report templates that have been embedded in the Notes application can be made available to users by just adding Action buttons in the Notes application. Consider the scenario where an employee needs to create time-sheet reports from an HR application. Using IntelliPRINT, the reports can be triggered by 'action' buttons within the application, and directly mailed to users as PDF attachments.

The entire process can be automated on a Domino server using Notes agents that can generate reports automatically at pre-defined intervals, e.g. weekly reports that are generated every Monday. The agent will also handle emailing of these reports to the users.

Automation of the entire reporting system for scheduled reporting provides tremendous benefits to IT personnel as well as the business users. IT no longer needs to spend days working on manual report creation and business users are guaranteed timely delivery of reports.

Creating a Simple Report Using the Wizard

With IntelliPRINT Reporting, simple tabular reports can be created in a matter of minutes. The procedure below describes the steps involved in creating a simple report. The steps below are to be performed on the Pinnacle Electronics sample database provided with IntelliPRINT Reporting. The database is automatically installed while installing IntelliPRINT Reporting.

To create a simple report using a wizard:

1. Open the Formats list in IntelliPRINT Reporting – Designer, via the Notes Actions menu.

2. Click **New** and choose **Report**. Select the **Standard Report Wizard**.

3. In the Report Wizard, use the **Edit Database** button to define the database from which the report needs to be generated. Click **Edit query** to start the visual query builder. Select the required fields from the Views listed.

4. Select the page layout and the report style, and you're done.

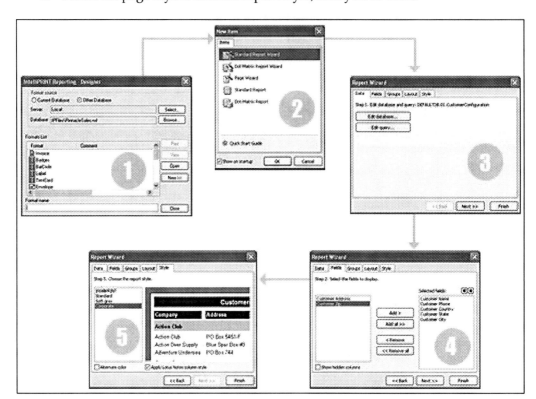

And you're report is ready; the Wizard will now place the bands automatically. Click the **Preview** button to view the final report. You can even adjust the band layout to suit your needs. The entire process takes just a few minutes!

Creating a Complex Report with IntelliPRINT Reporting

IntelliPRINT Reporting allows you to create a variety of complex reports such as:

- Master-detail reports
- Multi-database reports
- Subreports
- Parameterized reports
- Cross-tab reports
- Charts

Here we will step through the procedure for creating a Master-Detail report; we'll be working with the Pinnacle Electronics sample database that is provided with IntelliPRINT Reporting.

A Master-Detail report connects to a database using multiple queries. The idea is to extract related information from two different queries and print them in the same report. For instance, we can design a report which utilizes two queries - the first query fetches the customer Name and ID while the second query extracts the same customer's purchase details, such as the Product name, Quantity and Unit price.

To create a Master-Detail report:

1. Open the database from which the report has to be generated. IntelliPRINT Reporting will now use this as the default database automatically.

2. Open the Formats list in IntelliPRINT Reporting – Designer, via the Notes Actions menu.

3. Click **New** and choose **Report**. Cancel the **Standard Report Wizard** as we'll be designing this report manually.

4. Add a Notes database connection by selecting **Insert | LN Database** from the menu. A new icon named **LNDatabase1** should appear in Data pane (at the bottom).

5. Define a Notes query by selecting **Insert | LN Query** from the menu. A new icon named **LNQuery1** should appear in Data pane. Repeat this step to add **LNQuery2**.

6. Double-click **LNQuery1** to open the Query Builder window, seen below. Expand the View that contains the required fields, and drag the appropriate fields' folder to the Data Fields box to populate it with the list of fields. LNQuery1 is ready. Similarly, define LNQuery2.

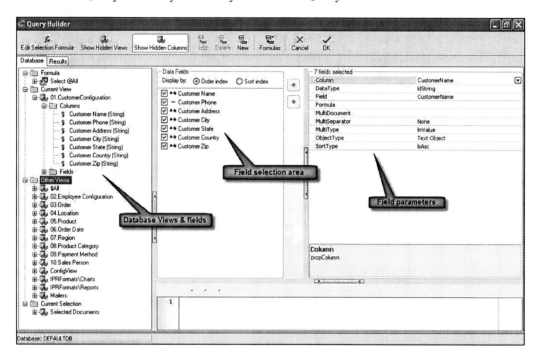

7. Insert the Master Band by selecting **Insert | Insert Band | Master Data** from the menu options. Use LNQuery1 in the **Select DataSet** dialog box.

8. Insert a Detail Band by selecting **Insert | Insert Band | Detail Data** from the menu options. Use LNQuery2 this time in the **Select DataSet** dialog box.

9. Now you can add the required fields from the Data Tree window (on the right side). Just drag and drop the field to the Master and Detail bands

10. Add a **Report Title** band and define the title as **Master Detail Report**.

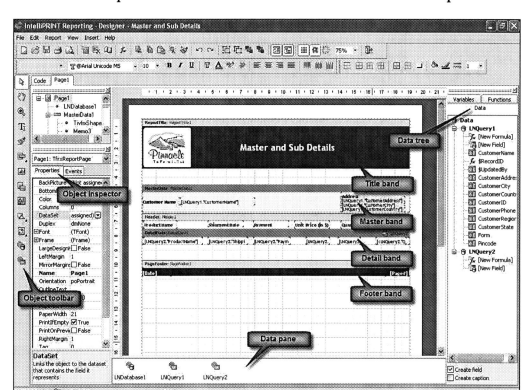

Your report is ready, click **Preview** to view your report. To add even more power to your report, you can add objects such as Computed Columns, Images, Charts, Cross-tab tables, Rich Text, Sub report objects, and a lot more.

Conclusion

To sum up, here's why IntelliPRINT Reporting can help you improve the productivity of your reporting system:

- Shortened report development cycle
- Superior performance because of its native 'designed-for-Notes' approach
- Advanced drag-and-drop and wizard-based reporting functionality
- Presentation-quality reports that are print-ready as well
- Support for native Notes features, including the Notes security framework

All of these make IntelliPRINT Reporting the product of choice for reporting and printing with Lotus Notes and Domino applications.

For more information on IntelliPRINT, please visit `http://www.synaptris.com/go/intelliprint`.

IONET Incremental Archiver

IONET are a Wellington, New Zealand based company that have specialised in Lotus Notes and Domino solutions since v3.0. They concentrate on innovative, low-cost products to enhance the usability of any Lotus Notes/Domino environment.

For a demonstration copy of the Incremental Archiver, or more information on IONET or our products, please visit `http://www.ionetsoftware.com`.

The IONET Incremental Archiver complements R8 as an automatic archive/restore tool for Lotus Notes data. In the Archiver, we use standard Lotus Notes technologies, but in an innovative way, which is the focus of this article.

Briefly, the Archiver automatically installs, archives, allows users to restore document versions and deletions themselves, and removes production data (including mail). It does this via a combination of Notes replication and a host of other functions that may be useful for any Notes/Domino environment. Coupled with the usability of R8, this makes a powerful platform for your archiving requirements.

The Archiver has been designed to allow users to restore their own data from any date (including document versions), using the source Notes application they are familiar with, be it mail or any other Notes database. This means that the hierarchy of the data (e.g. responses) is preserved and therefore familiar to the user. It also means that the IT Department no longer has to juggle backup tapes to restore user data. The user can also search Archives, providing a 'back-through-time' look at document versions in the Archive.

All facets of the Archiving process are automatically enabled and controlled by the Administrator, Notes security is observed, and full backups can still be taken for Disaster Recovery. In addition, Notes databases no longer need custom Archiving solutions, as data can be simply deleted from the database and remains in the Archive, including document versions. That means you can safely use the 'Remove documents not modified in the last x days' setting to control database size (the Archiver can also remove documents for you according to combinations of dates and @formulas). For the full product description, features and downloads, please visit `http://www.ionetsoftware.com/archiving`.

Let's have a look at the main components in more detail. They are:

- **Setup Archiving**: Create the Archiving environment per database
- **The Archive Process**: Locate, Compress, Archive and Remove Data
- **The Restore Process**: View Actions
- **Searching Archive**: Including Search functions i.e. Client JS

Setup Archiving

To make it easier to administer, the Archiver installation is automated as much as possible. The setup process below is followed for each database included in the Archive:

1. Add three design elements (an Agent, View and Form) to the production database design. This is performed using the excellent DBDesign LotusScript class from Damien Katz (ex. IRIS). This class treats Notes Design elements as Notes Documents, thus allowing them to be copied between databases using the `CopyToDatabase` NotesDocument method. This library is available via the Sandbox on the Lotus Developers Domain.

2. Create a replica on the Archive Server. This is performed using the `CreateReplica` method.

3. Set the Replica to not replicate deletions, via the `NotesReplication` LotusScript class.

4. Set the Replica to only replicate documents matching a user-defined @ formula, using the `NotesReplicationEntry` LotusScript class.

5. Create a copy of the newly created replica on the Archive Server (this copy contains document versions). This is performed using the `CreateCopy` method of the NotesDatabase class.

6. Check there is no scheduled replication (by trawling Directory documents), and that the Replica cannot write back to the Production database (via NotesACL LotusScript methods). These checks are also performed before each Archiving operation to ensure the integrity of data.

7. Create Full Text Indices of the newly created databases on the Archive Server. This function is not directly possible via LotusScript. However, it is possible to create a separate LotusScript agent (called BuildIndex) that opens a database locally (using " as the server argument) and creates an Index using the `CreateFTIndex` method of the NotesDatabase class. Using a second agent, you then instantiate this agent and call the RunOnServer method, passing a NotesDocument containing the database information. The result is to create a Full Text Index on the Server. This is shown below.

Calling the BuildIndex Agent

```
Sub Initialize

    Dim s As New NotesSession
    Dim db As NotesDatabase
    Dim agent As NotesAgent
    Dim doc As NotesDocument

    Set db = s.CurrentDatabase
    Set doc = ... Set the document object containing the Database
Replica ID
    Set agent = db.GetAgent("BuildIndex")
    Call agent.RunOnServer(doc.NoteID)

End Sub
```

BuildIndex Agent

```
Sub Initialize

    Dim s As New NotesSession
    Dim db As NotesDatabase
    Dim targetDB As New NotesDatabase("", "")
    Dim agent As NotesAgent
    Dim doc As NotesDocument

    Set db = s.CurrentDatabase
    Set agent = s.CurrentAgent
    Set doc = db.GetDocumentByID(agent.ParameterDocID)
    If Not (doc Is Nothing) Then
            replicaID$ = doc.DBReplicaID(0)
            If targetDB.OpenByReplicaID("", replicaID$) Then
                    Call targetDB.CreateFTIndex(23, False)
            End If
    End If

End Sub
```

The Archive Process

During setup, we created a replica on the Archive Server (the Archive Replica) and a copy of that replica (the Archive Store), for each production database.

A scheduled agent in the Archiver checks each Production database for any changes made to eligible documents (i.e. those matching the Archive @formula for the Database) since the last time replication occurred, using the Search method of the NotesDatabase class - the Search method allows reasonable search performance using time/date criteria within databases that may or may not be Full Text Indexed.

For any document that has been modified, the corresponding document is located in the Archive Replica (where it contains the previous content). This document is copied to the Archive Store database. Because we're copying data on the same file system and not traversing a network, this is a reasonably fast process.

During the copy process, the user has the choice to automatically ZIP attachments. This is done by calling a Java agent that uses the java.util.zip package. Briefly, the steps are:

1. Make an array of all eligible attachments in the document and write this to the document.

2. Extract the attachments to disk and remove them from the document.

3. Call the Java agent, again using the NotesAgent RunOnServer method and passing the document NoteID. The Java agent locates the files on disk according to information in the document, ZIPs them, then writes a flag once finished. The initial agent sees the flag and reattaches the ZIP files to the document.

Calling the Java Agent

```
Set doc = ... Set the document object containing information on the
files to ZIP
Call session.SetEnvironmentVar("ZipAgentStatus","")
Set agent = db.GetAgent("(ZipFiles)")
Call agent.RunOnServer(doc.NoteID)
chkFinished$ = session.GetEnvironmentString("ZipAgentStatus")
While chkFinished$ = ""
    chkFinished$ = session.GetEnvironmentString("ZipAgentStatus")
    Sleep 1
Wend
```

The ZipFiles Java Agent

```
import lotus.domino.*;
import java.io.*;
import java.util.*;
import java.util.zip.*;
import java.text.*;
```

```
public class JavaAgent extends AgentBase {

    private ZipInputStream inZipFile;
    private String aDBServer;
    private String aDBFileName;
    private String aDBNoteID;
    private String zipFileNameInput;
    private String zipFileNameOutput;

public void NotesMain() {
    try {
            Session session = getSession(); //Instantiate NotesSession
            AgentContext agentContext = session.getAgentContext();
            //Instantiate AgentContext
            Database db = agentContext.getCurrentDatabase();
            //Instantiate CurrentDatabase
            Agent agent = agentContext.getCurrentAgent();
            //Instantiate CurrentAgent
            Document callingDoc =
            db.getDocumentByID(agent.getParameterDocID());
            //Get the doc calling this agent
            String aDBServer = callingDoc.getItemValueString
            ("IOZipDBServer"); //Get the server of the target database
            String aDBFileName = callingDoc.getItemValueString
            ("IOZipDBFileName"); //Get the filename of the target
             database
            String aDBNoteID = callingDoc.getItemValueString
            ("IOZipNoteID"); //Get the Note ID of the target document
            Database aDB = session.getDatabase(aDBServer, aDBFileName);
            //Open the target database
            Document doc = aDB.getDocumentByID(aDBNoteID);
            //Get the target document
            Vector zipFileInput = doc.getItemValue("IOZipInput");
            //Source uncompressed files
            Vector zipFileOutput = doc.getItemValue("IOZipOutput");
            //Target compressed files

            byte[] buffer = new byte[18024];

            for (int i = 0; i < zipFileInput.size(); i++) {
                // Associate a file input stream for the current file
                String zipFileNameOutput = (String)zipFileOutput.
                elementAt(i);
                ZipOutputStream out = new ZipOutputStream(new
                FileOutputStream(zipFileNameOutput));
                out.setLevel(Deflater.DEFAULT_COMPRESSION);
                String zipFileNameInput =
                  (String)zipFileInput.elementAt(i);
```

```
                    FileInputStream in = new
                    FileInputStream(zipFileNameInput);
                    // Add ZIP entry to output stream.
                    out.putNextEntry(new ZipEntry(zipFileNameInput));
                    int len;
                    while ((len = in.read(buffer)) > 0) {
                            out.write(buffer, 0, len);
                    }
                    // Close the current entry
                    out.closeEntry();
                    // Close the current file input stream
                    in.close();
                    out.close();
                }
                session.setEnvironmentVar("ZipAgentStatus",
                "Completed", false);
                session.recycle();
                agentContext.recycle();
                db.recycle();
                agent.recycle();
                doc.recycle();
                }
                catch (IllegalArgumentException iae) {
                        iae.printStackTrace();
                }
                catch (FileNotFoundException fnfe) {
                        fnfe.printStackTrace();
                }
                catch (IOException ioe) {
                        ioe.printStackTrace();
                }
                catch(Exception e) {
                        e.printStackTrace();
                }
        }
    }
```

When all eligible documents have been zipped and copied, the agent initiates normal Notes replication between the Production Database and Archive Replica to update the Archive Replica. It does this via the Replicate method of the NotesDatabase class.

So by identifying modified documents BEFORE they are updated via replication, an accurate versioning of the documents is achieved.

Because deletions are not replicated to the Archive Replica, all documents are permanently retained. Replication and ACL settings are verified before every Archive procedure to ensure deletions are not replicated back into Production when deletion stubs have been purged.

The final part of the Archive process is to remove documents from the Production database, if they match the criteria specified for the database, using a combination of document age, last accessed date, last modified date, and @formulas.

The Restore Process

During the setup process, a Dialogbox Form and a 'Restore Document' Agent are automatically added to the Production database. When a user wants to restore a document, they run this agent. They are prompted for the date and it is retrieved from either the Archive Replica or Archive Store (depending on the required date), and opened.

The following graphics show the Restore operation. Note the handy use of the R8 function to modify the right-hand menu.

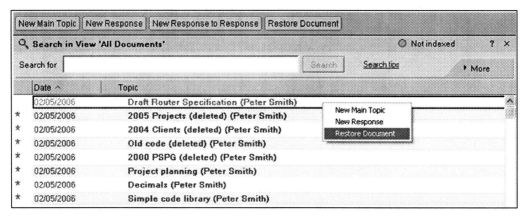

The user then has to select the type of Restore:

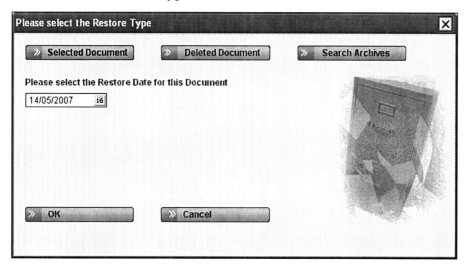

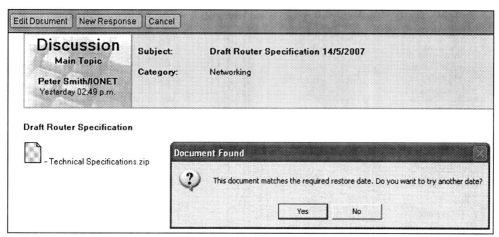

If the user wants to restore a deleted document, they instead automatically open the Archive Replica (where deletions are not removed), locate the document they want, set the date and repeat the restore process, retrieving the document from either the Archive Replica or Archive Store depending on the required date. Users can then restore deleted documents to the Production database.

The user is also able to search the Archive Replica and Archive Store databases for the data they want.

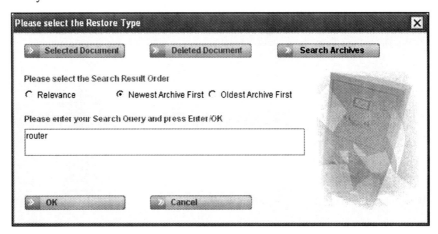

This allows a 'back through time' search facility that includes the date archived. This functionality is provided via our FT Search Manager, which allows simultaneous searching of multiple Full Text Indices.

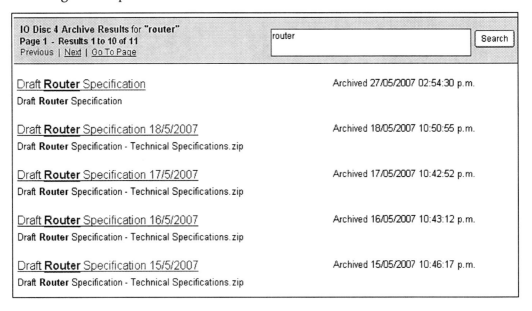

Conclusion

Housekeeping agents optionally clear out Archived data after a configurable period.

A separate database option allows the restore process to use a separate directory, so that if a restore of data from 5 years ago is required, the Archive Replica and Archive Store tape backups can be restored into this directory and the process works from there instead of the normal location. This is so that 'normal' full backups to tape can be performed if required (i.e. for Disaster Recovery, reducing disk space usage etc.)

Another benefit of the Archiver is that no other form of archiving is required (i.e. no custom data archives need be done by the IT Department), documents can be simply deleted from the Production database and they will remain available in the Archive Replica for restore.

CMT Inspector for Lotus Notes

Your Domino infrastructure gets more complex every day, and effectively managing through that complexity can save your firm time and money. Before making upgrades/additions/wholesale changes to your Domino environment, gain the knowledge you need regarding what legacy applications exist today, with granular information on critical metrics such as usage, access and attachments. Easily identify opportunities for improved storage and security policies based on real-world results that point to changed business needs, falling usage/access, etc. CMT Inspector provides the inspection and analysis you need to not only justify the legacy environment, but also effectively plan for future investment options. CMT Inspector provides the following functionalities:

- Usage Reports
- Security Reports
- Server Statistics
- Email Statistics
- Code Search and Comparison
- Content Analysis
- Application Design Analysis
- User Surveys
- Application Template Matching
- Notes Upgrade Validation
- Extensive Code Validation Rules Engine
- Code Flowcharting

- Export to Access

- Design Sophistication Indexes

- Express and Advanced Settings

- Usage Analysis

- Redundant Failover Logic

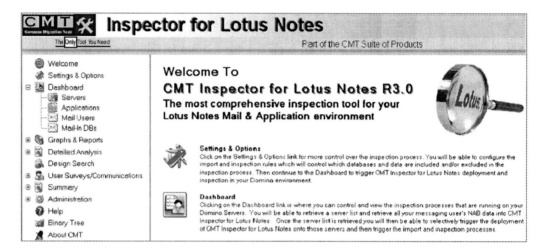

Will You Code Break When You Upgrade?

CMT Inspector contains an extensive Rules Filtering Engine with hundreds of rules that can be leveraged to find out if your applications will work when you upgrade. These rules can be modified and updated based on your environment. Furthermore, unlike simple searching that is performed by other products, CMT Inspector Rules can be tied to code snippets which can be executed to give you an even better understanding of the code in your Notes environment. This figure shows the Code Inspector at work:

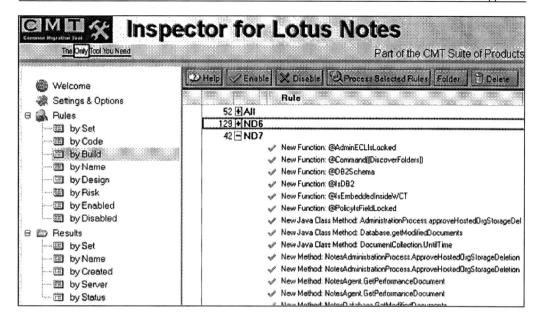

Design Search, User Surveys and Flowcharting

CMT Inspector for Lotus offers you the capability to search for specific keywords across all design elements in your Lotus Notes Applications in order to identify specific functionality that you may want to uncover.

User surveys can be configured, distributed, and reported on to gather useful information from the application's users. Surveys can be delivered to document authors/edits or based on who is in the ACL.

All code can be flowcharted and exported to Visio for much better analysis.

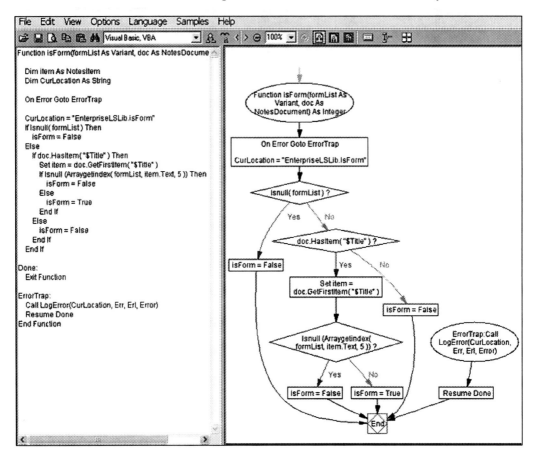

Reports and Export

CMT Inspector comes with an extensive collection of reports that can be automatically generated. Furthermore, all data can be exported to Microsoft Access for further reporting and querying. This means that almost any report can be generated on the fly.

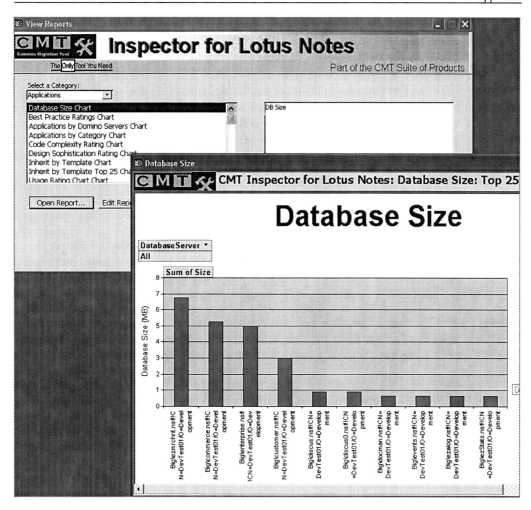

CMT for Public Folders

You have business-critical information stored in Exchange Public Folders. You have to migrate to Lotus Notes, but, how do you migrate the data in the Public Folders?

Making your mail migrations from Microsoft Exchange to Lotus Domino easier is a snap with Binary Tree's CMT for Public Folders. This solution provides a simple and user-friendly means of migrating a public folder hierarchy to a single database.

The data in a Microsoft Exchange Public Folder often has significant value that has been protected with permissions, based on the identity stores in Exchange's Directory. CMT for Exchange Public folders was created to help companies recover the intellectual capital often found in Public Folders. CMT not only takes data from the Public Folders, but can also mimic the permissions that existed on the Exchange servers in brand new Domino databases. CMT migrates the standard Exchange document types, including mail messages, calendar events, journal items, tasks and notes. If your Public Folders contain forms that have been modified to include additional fields and data types, the CMT tool can be customized to migrate this data, as well.

CMT for Notes

The Binary Tree Common Migration Tool (CMT) migrates data from one email system to another. The tool can be used to migrate from numerous email systems to Lotus Notes, and like the DUS tool, CMT has the ability to migrate both Server-Based data and end-user based data.

Binary Tree's Common Migration Tool for Notes builds on 14 years of outstanding email and calendar/schedule migration solutions from Binary Tree. To date, millions of users world-wide have been migrated to Lotus Notes with Binary Tree's CMT for Notes tool.

CMT for Notes offers several business benefits:

- Enterprise migration solution that can manage large migrations (up to 50,000 users have been migrated at one time). There is no limit to the number of users that can be imported from a source directory.
- Wizards set up specific functions such as importing users, registration to the Domino directory, the end-user migration and the server-to-server migration.
- Ability to create mail files during the registration process.
- Date filtering for migrating mail, calendar and tasks during an Exchange server-to-server migration.
- Process can be rolled out into two steps: user registration and user migration.
- Customize data types for migration, including mail, calendar, notes, journal, tasks and contacts, depending on individual needs, space and time.
- Schedule users and/or groups to migrate at specific times, thereby limiting network load and support calls.
- Migrations do not require end-users. The Administrator can perform the migration, cutting down on your IT department's time and expense.
- Detailed logs with extensive error reporting help administrators identify, interpret and resolve issues.

CMT for Coexistence

By off-loading most of the traffic from the Microsoft Exchange Notes Connector, Binary Tree's CMT for Coexistence yields a more stable and reliable connection between Lotus Notes and Microsoft Exchange.

The most popular and highly functional connectivity solution between Microsoft Exchange and Lotus Notes environments is the Notes Connector for Microsoft Exchange. This solution addresses e-mail, calendar, scheduling and task data exchange, automated directory synchronization and free/busy lookup between Microsoft Exchange and Lotus Notes environments.

To overcome issues reported by many customers using the Microsoft Notes Connector, Binary Tree's solution greatly enhances fidelity of mail exchange and improves connectivity reliability. This is accomplished by a series of configuration and programmatic changes in the environment.

iCal is supported with the advent of Exchange 2000 and Notes 6. iCal is the standard for the encoding of a calendar messages in SMTP format. This allows email and calendaring to be sent via SMTP, which greatly decreases the stress on the Microsoft Connector, improving data fidelity.

What does CMT for Lotus/Exchange Coexistence do?

CMT for Coexistence offloads all mail traffic from the Microsoft Notes Connector using SMTP and MIME encoding, effectively bypassing the inefficient Rich Text conversion used by the Microsoft Exchange Notes Connector. Mime encoding is much more efficient, preserving 100% fidelity.

CMT for Coexistence offloads all calendar traffic by encoding the message in iCal format and passing it via SMTP, instead of through the Microsoft Notes Connector.

What does the Microsoft Notes Connector do when Integrated with CMT for Lotus/Exchange Coexistence?

- Directory Synchronization
- Free/Busy Lookups

- Never crash and have the ability to scale to an unlimited amount of users

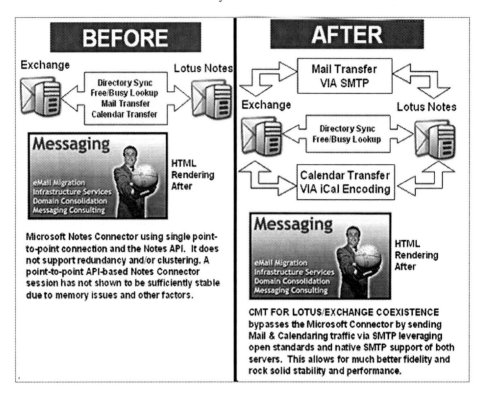

CMT for Domains

Your Domain infrastructure is a vital asset, and one that should be protected. Your IT environment is unique, which means that you need something designed with adaptability in mind.

Enter Binary Tree's CMT for Domains, Users, Servers and Desktops, a solution which expedites the conversion between platforms, while diminishing the impact on your IT resources. A user-friendly administrator tool requiring virtually no end-user interaction, CMT for Domains, Servers, Users and Desktops will enable you to automate the entire migration lifecycle in minutes.

Utilizing CMT for Domains, Servers, Users and Desktops, the following processes can be accomplished with the click of a button:

- **Entire Environment and User Audit**: Wholly automates the replacement of users' present naming structure to the new one.

- **All-encompassing Jurisdiction of the Migration Process**: Grants the Administrator a complete overview of the migration life-cycle, providing meticulous data with process information based on migration phases or users.

- **Instigates the re-name of multiple users to the new hierarchical name/upgrade**: The practice of migrating and/or consolidating Lotus Notes Domains is habitually escorted by altering end-users' hierarchical naming structures. Commonly, a Lotus Notes Administrator performs the process of Lotus Notes Domain migration by using a multifaceted, lingering process provided by Lotus. CMT for Domains, Users, Servers and Desktops condenses this process, accomplishing the task quickly and efficiently, but with the minimal amount of effort.

- **Notes Desktop Update**: Programmed as an email message containing a button for each user to click, users' desktop information (server names for databases, user accesses, mail file and personal address book, location documents, connection documents, etc.) are automatically updated to the new infrastructure information with one click.

- **Notes Port**: Runs on the Domino server and by design, replaces all reference to each migrated user's old infrastructure information with the new one in the users mail database. (Includes fields in mail messages, calendar, meetings and to-dos)

Additionally, you can:

- Move users/applications to a different Notes Domain/Domino Server and amend the Domino Directory to reflect the move

- Monitor the rename process

- Monitor the move Progress

- Forget about digging through help files looking for answers

Never before has a consolidation of multiple Lotus Notes Domains been more straight-forward. CMT for Domains, Users, Servers and Desktops consists of everything a Lotus Notes Administrator needs to move users from an existing domain to a new one. Furthermore, as a result of the migration using CMT, users will appear to have always lived on the new domain.

Index

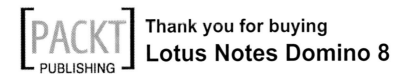

Thank you for buying
Lotus Notes Domino 8

About Packt Publishing

Packt, pronounced 'packed', published its first book *"Mastering phpMyAdmin for Effective MySQL Management"* in April 2004 and subsequently continued to specialize in publishing highly focused books on specific technologies and solutions.

Our books and publications share the experiences of your fellow IT professionals in adapting and customizing today's systems, applications, and frameworks. Our solution based books give you the knowledge and power to customize the software and technologies you're using to get the job done. Packt books are more specific and less general than the IT books you have seen in the past. Our unique business model allows us to bring you more focused information, giving you more of what you need to know, and less of what you don't.

Packt is a modern, yet unique publishing company, which focuses on producing quality, cutting-edge books for communities of developers, administrators, and newbies alike. For more information, please visit our website: www.packtpub.com.

Writing for Packt

We welcome all inquiries from people who are interested in authoring. Book proposals should be sent to authors@packtpub.com. If your book idea is still at an early stage and you would like to discuss it first before writing a formal book proposal, contact us; one of our commissioning editors will get in touch with you.

We're not just looking for published authors; if you have strong technical skills but no writing experience, our experienced editors can help you develop a writing career, or simply get some additional reward for your expertise.

Upgrading to Lotus Notes and Domino 7

ISBN: 1-904811-63-9   Paperback: 320 pages

Upgrade your company to the latest version of Lotus Notes and Domino.

1. Understand the new features and put them to work in your business

2. Appreciate the implications of changes and new features

3. Learn how to integrate Lotus Notes/Domino 7 with WebSphere and Microsoft Outlook

4. A real-life case study of how Lotus upgraded its own developerWorks site to Lotus Notes/ Domino 7

Zimbra

ISBN: 978-1-847192-08-0   Paperback: 220 pages

Get your organization up and running with Zimbra, fast

1. Get your organization up and running with Zimbra, fast

2. Administer the Zimbra server and work with the Zimbra web client

3. Protect your Zimbra installation from hackers, spammers, and viruses

4. Access Zimbra from Microsoft Outlook

Please check **www.PacktPub.com** for information on our titles

Printed in the United States
107527LV00005B/147-148/A

9 781847 192745